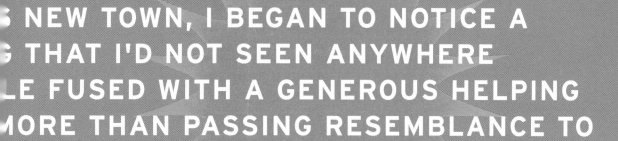

 NEW TOWN, I BEGAN TO NOTICE A
 THAT I'D NOT SEEN ANYWHERE
L FUSED WITH A GENEROUS HELPING
MORE THAN PASSING RESEMBLANCE TO

PRET TY VACAN T

CLIVE PIERCY

PRETTY VACANT

THE LOS ANGELES *Dingbat* OBSERVED

CHRONICLE BOOKS

SAN FRANCISCO

Library of Congress Cataloging-in-Publication Data available.

ISBN 0-8118-4024-7

Manufactured in China

BOOK DESIGN BY Ph.D

Distributed in Canada by Raincoast Books
9050 Shaughnessy Street
Vancouver, British Columbia V6P 6E5

10 9 8 7 6 5 4 3 2 1

Chronicle Books LLC
85 Second Street
San Francisco, California 94105

www.chroniclebooks.com

for the amazing ann field and the sublime ray piercy

I moved to Los Angeles from London in 1982. Although I'd never been here before, the city was instantly familiar to me, for somewhere deep inside me lurked the spirits of Raymond Chandler and Nathanael West. Indeed, the biggest surprise to me, upon arrival, was that the city existed in glorious full color and not in black-and-white, for my impressions of it had been formed from Billy Wilder films and Max Yavno photographs. I'd read Reyner Banham's wonderful book **LOS ANGELES: The Architecture of Four Ecologies** and loved it, I think, because it took an outsider's point of view, he being a fellow Brit. It's funny how often an artist comes to a city from somewhere else and ends up representing that place more than a homegrown one does. In LA's case that's certainly true. David Hockney, from grim and grimy Bradford, and Ed Ruscha, from lonely Oklahoma, have become the quintessential Los Angeles artists. I'd coveted their work from afar, but having moved here, I quickly realized how vital their voices are to the character of this city.

Banham's enthusiastic earthy prose, his interest in both high and low art, and the clarity of his vision struck a chord with this young graphic designer. A who's-who list of modernist masters sprung from his pages, magical names . . . Gill, Wright, Schindler, Neutra, Lautner, Ellwood, Koenig, and Eames. I was eager to explore. And that's the thing about LA – accessibility. Not a single one of my friends in England had lived in a house designed by Sir

Christopher Wren or Sir John Vanbrugh, but here it was possible, through sheer proximity, to find yourself at a party given by a friend of a friend of a friend's analyst's nutritionist who just happened to live in a little gem of an early Neutra.

I desperately needed somewhere to live. Trying to look as inconspicuous as possible in my Dodgers T-shirt and plastic Mickey Mouse ears, a partly finished screenplay tossed casually on the backseat of my turquoise-and-white '59 Nash Metropolitan and *(The Very Best of) Christopher Cross* blaring from the car radio, my wife and I began scouring the city for a suitable, (i.e., affordable) apartment. As we drove around our glamorous new town, I began to notice a certain type of apartment building that I'd not seen anywhere before. A purist international style fused with a generous helping of googie, some of them bearing a more than passing resemblance to Le Corbusier's Villa Savoye. Many of these structures sat precariously on rather thin stilts, a motley selection of Pintos, Chevettes, and Gremlins parked conveniently in the space below.

It was the architect Francis Ventre, I think, who coined the term "dingbats" for them, but they all began life as variations on the modernist stucco box that had effectively replaced, through economic necessity and postwar inventiveness, the Spanish colonial revival style that had dominated up until then. Structurally, that's what they consist of: generic boxes on three sides with all of the attention paid to the street facades. Sets. All surface and no depth. How apt is that for LA, I hear you scream. But how inventive those facades turn out to be. Some display admirable restraint – almost austere in some ways – while most reflect the exuberant optimism and confidence that were sweeping the country, and especially California, in the period from 1945 through to the early sixties. They seem to complement the consumer objects of the day, much more closely than at other moments in history, with their vibrant playful colors, organic-shaped details, and graphic patterns and textures afforded by the use of stucco. And at some point in the early fifties the garage doors disappeared from them, lightening the overall effect and making the carport and automobiles an integral part of the design. Was this because car design was going through its own creatively fertile period, too? Or, more likely, owing to bureaucratic zoning restrictions?

Not wishing to be outdone by their automobile counterparts, the stucco box designers adorned their buildings with an array of details. Many of the buildings have names, proudly displayed in script type on the facade. Some appear to be directly named after a loved one, like Debby Den, while many others evoke glamorous destinations, often Polynesian. But where do you aspire to go when you already live in Paradise, albeit Paradise with a lobotomy? In many cases the street numbers are audaciously out of proportion with the rest of the facade and, of course, as a typographer, these are favorites of mine. And perhaps most recognizable of all are the innumerable versions of dingbat light fixtures that, at night, make the buildings twinkle and glow.

Over the years I have documented these sadly beautiful buildings as I've driven around Los Angeles, mostly from the driver's-side window of my car. These snapshots – for that is all they were ever intended to be – are an attempt at conveying the curious life stories of these buildings, without ever showing any of the inhabitants. Today, those original cars have been replaced with equally ridiculous sounding counterparts: RAVs, Echos, Integras, and the saddest one of all, the Aspire. Parts of the name signage have dropped off, leaving us with tantalizing new ambiguities, so that "The Capri" has now become the much more contemporary sounding " he Cap ." And the street numbers have taken on a hardy patina. I return again and again to the same streets, just to make sure that these old friends of mine are still here, and I still feel a delicious sense of expectation when I turn on to a street and see an undiscovered dingbat in the distance. This is not a book about architecture – or photography. It is a visual poem, a love letter, and a simple attempt to help preserve these fantastic, quirky characters.

 CLIVE PIERCY

3665

STUDIO
APT.
W/VIEW

Deluxe

FIREPLACES • WET BARS
SOUNDPROOF

11728
KIOWA

Apartments

Sorry **NO VACANCY**

Villa

PLACES • CEN

DELUXE
1 & 2 BDRM. APTS.

PULLMAN BATHS
CARPETS - DRAPES
BUILT-IN GAS -
RANGE & OVEN
SOUNDPROOFING
PRIVATE PATIOS

1849 LELOIT

3415·19
Jasmine
Heated
POOL
Deluxe
APTS.
Sorry NO VACANCY

PAY ATTENTION THIS IS THE NEW LAW!
WARNING
NO DOGS
VIOLATORS WILL BE
POSITIVELY PROSECUTED
L.A.C.O. No. 8581

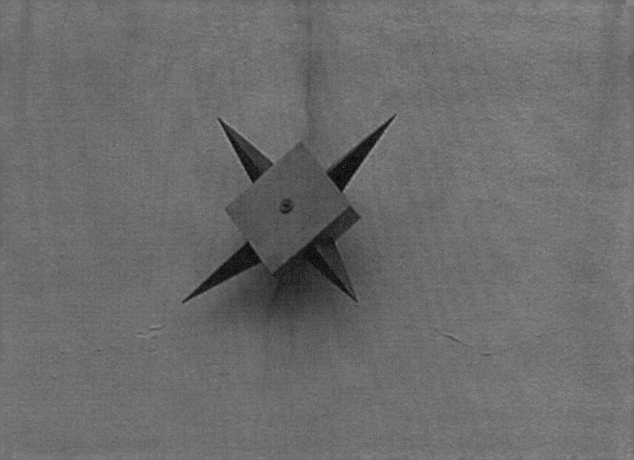

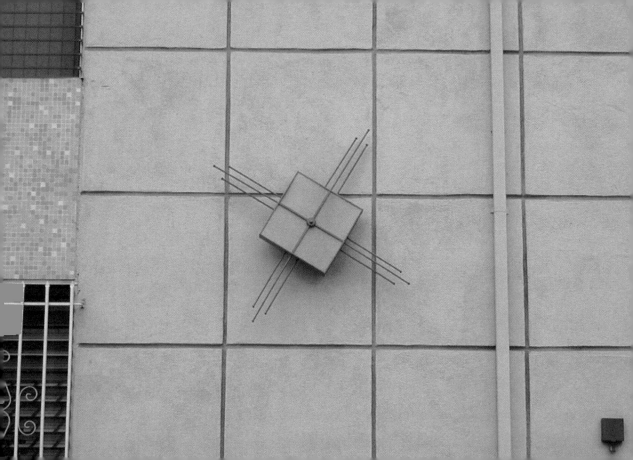

Edward Ruscha 1965

ED RUSCHA

BRONSON TROPICS

1965, GRAPHITE ON PAPER 14 1/8 x 22 5/8

1328

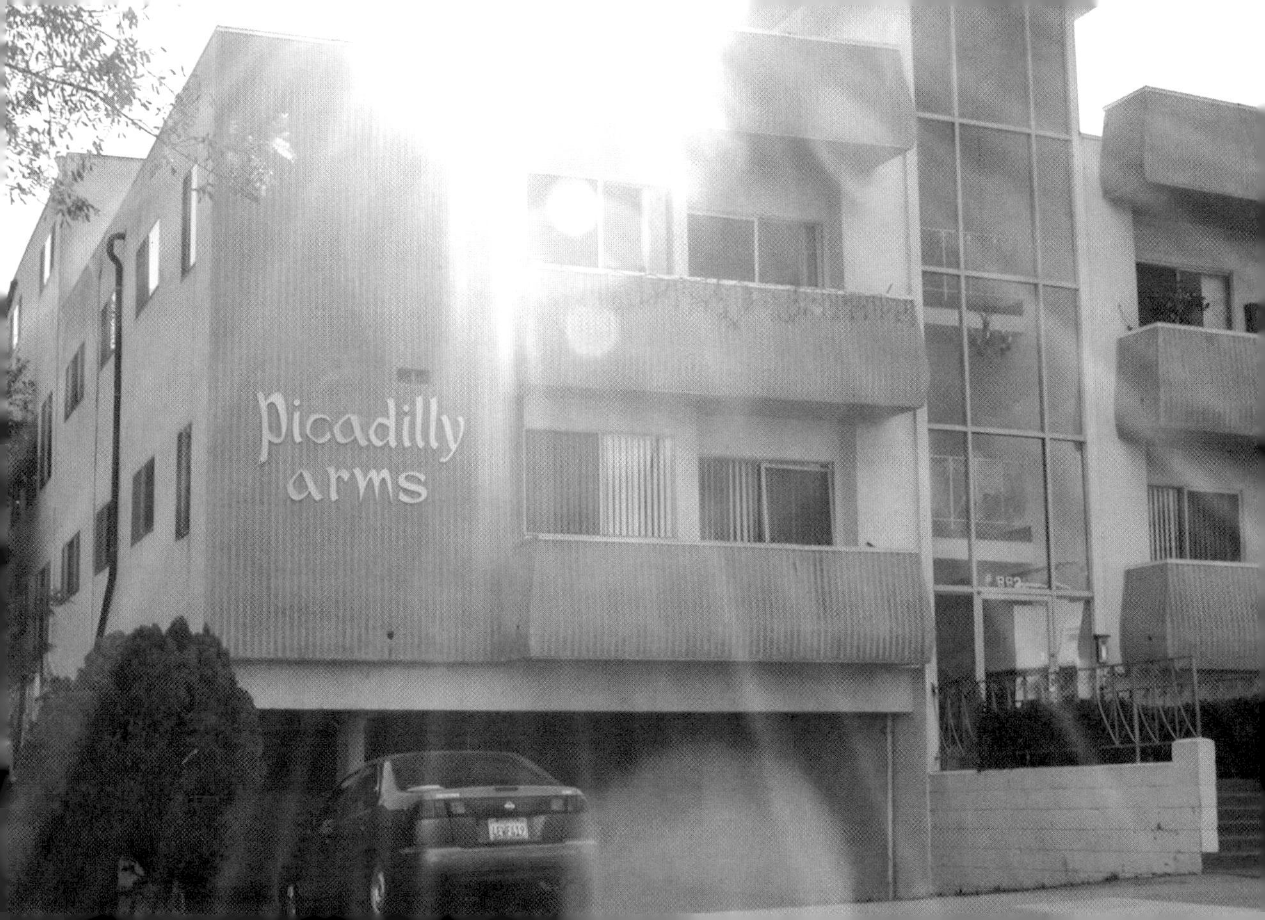
Picadilly
arms

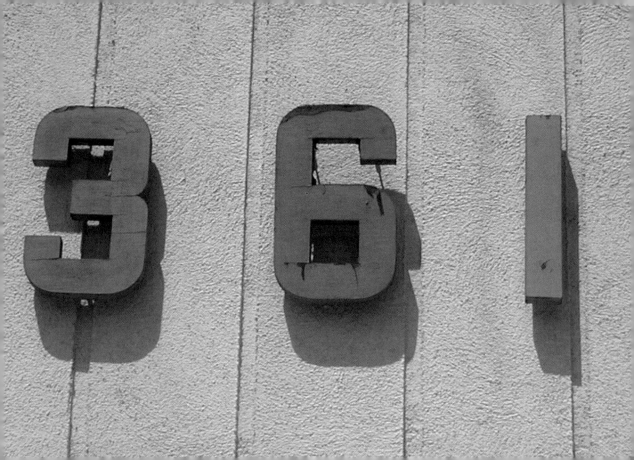

Eleven 'O' Two

Thirty

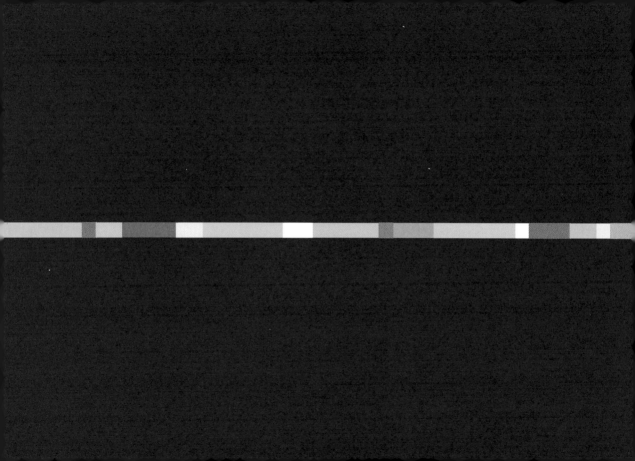

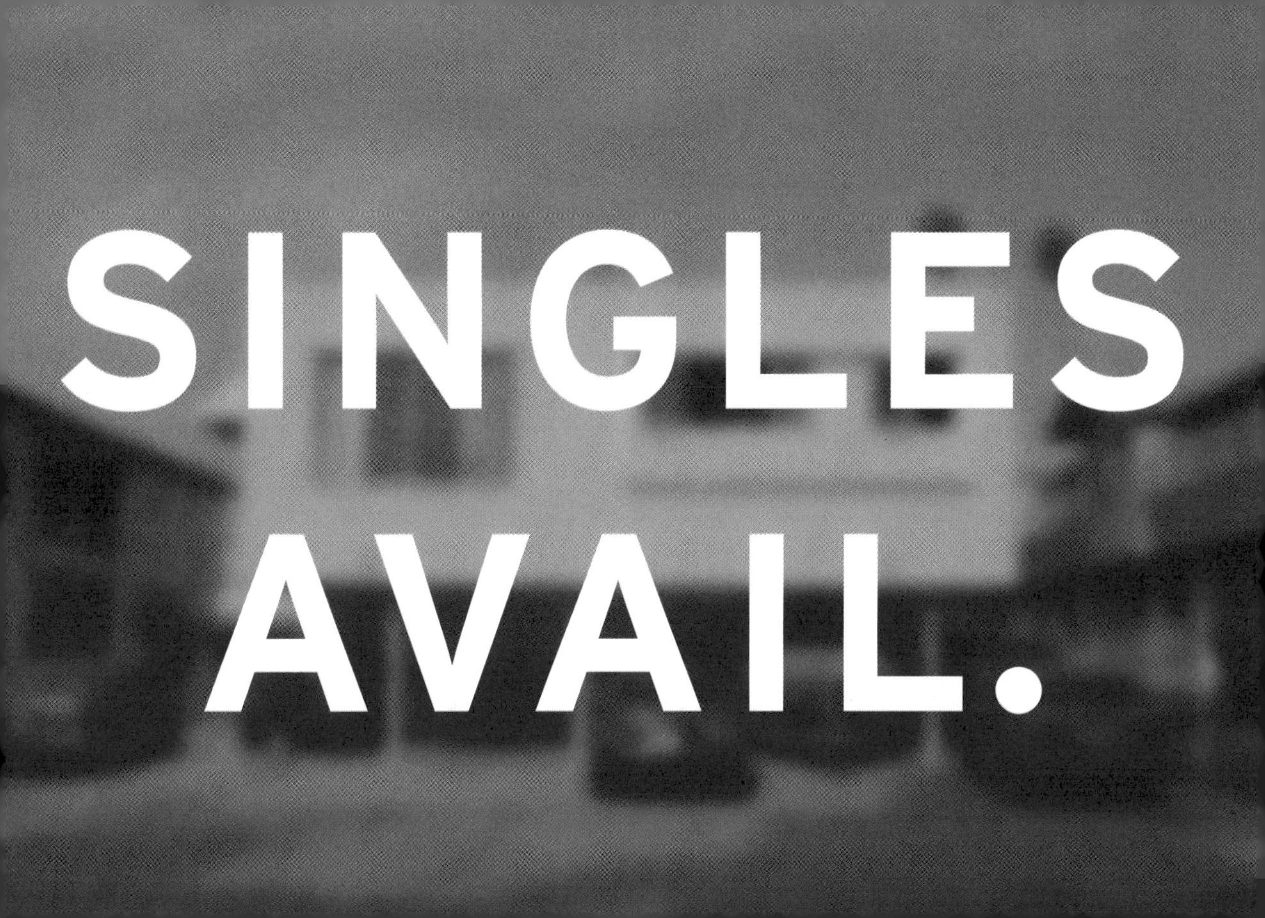
SINGLES
AVAIL.

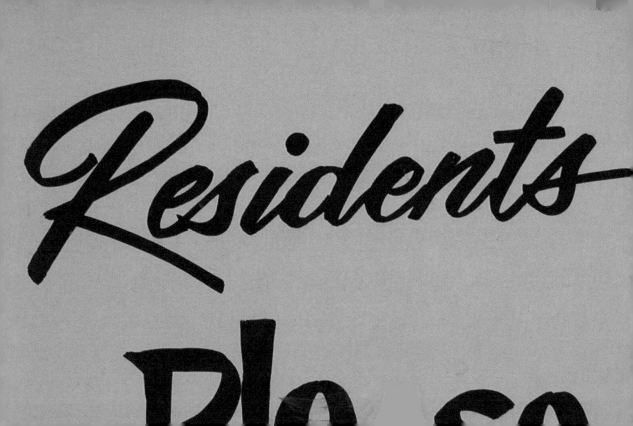

336 - 42 ½

NO PA

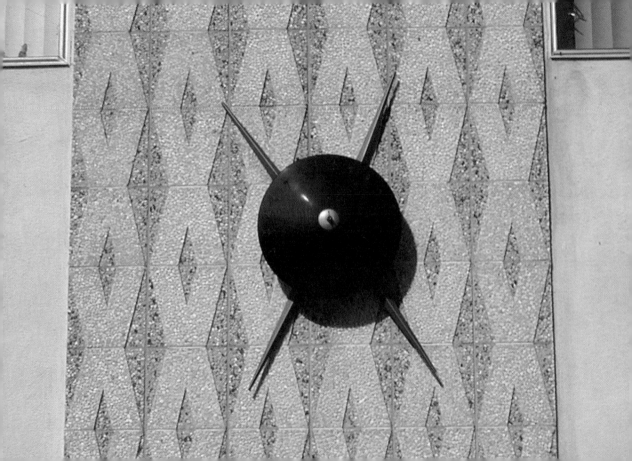

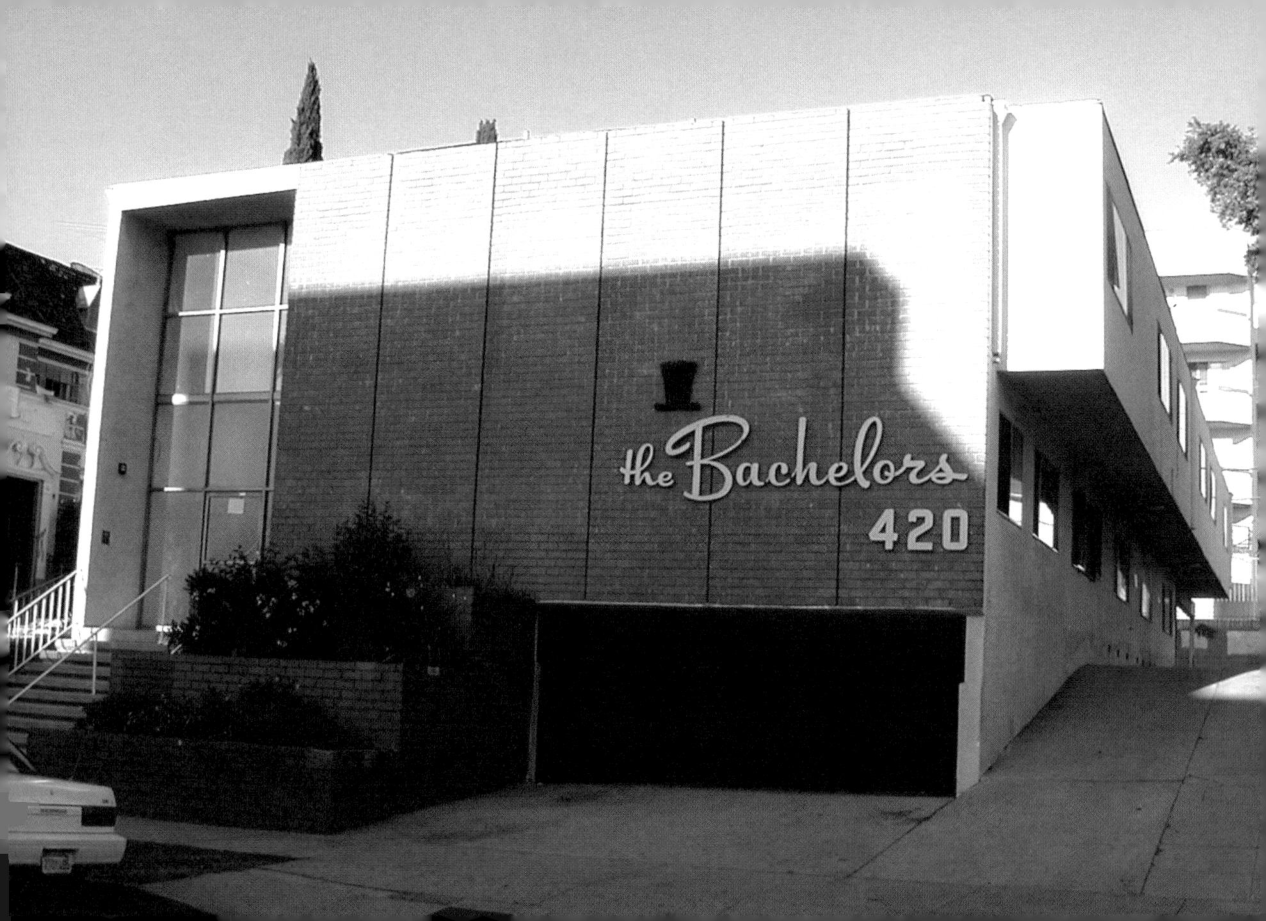
the Bachelors
420

11726

FOR LEASE
CENTURY WEST PROPERTIES
310/899-9580

SORRY, NO PETS

Riviera Villa

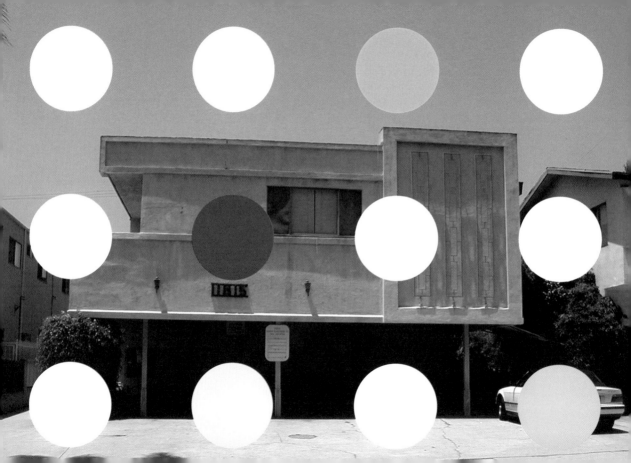

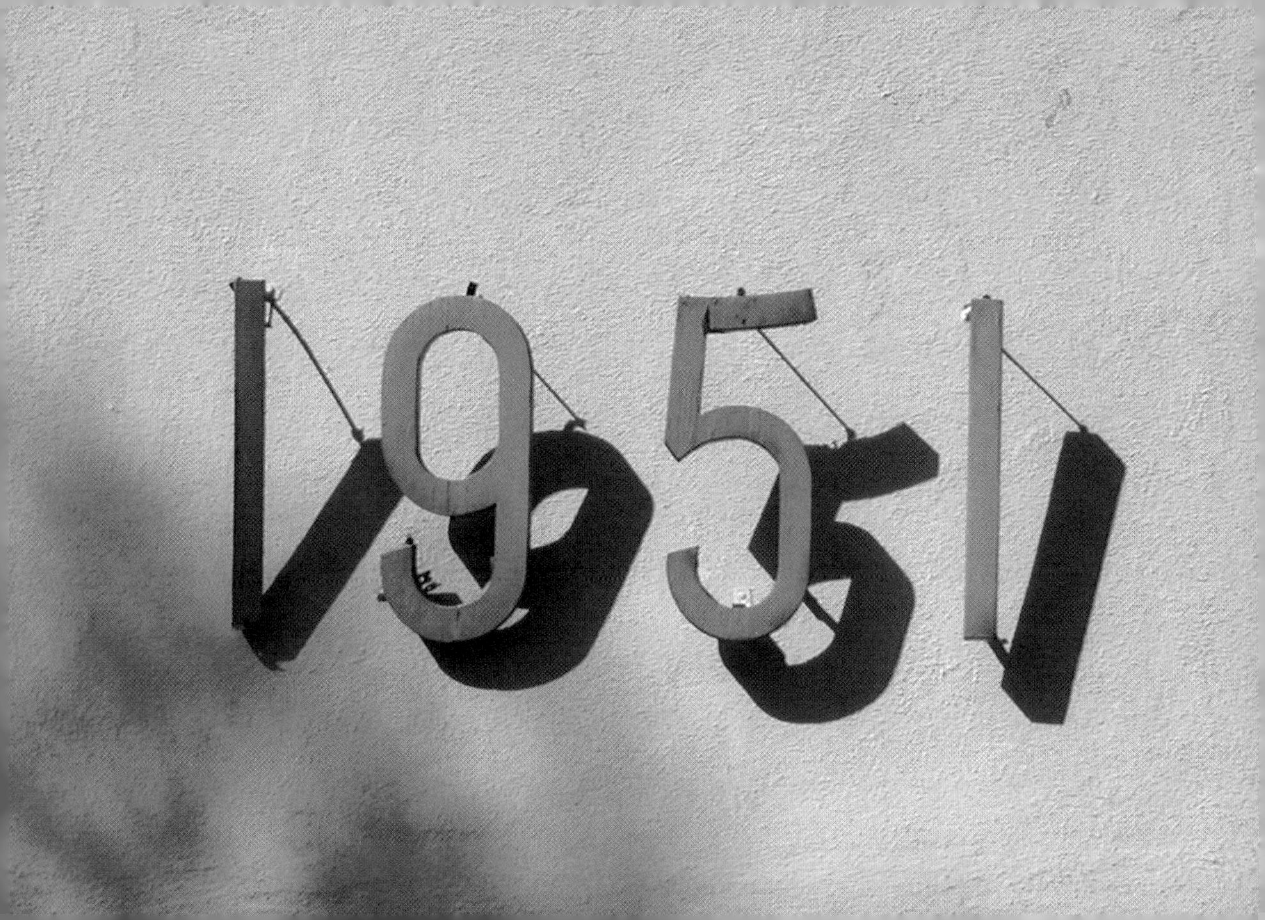
1951

1952

1953

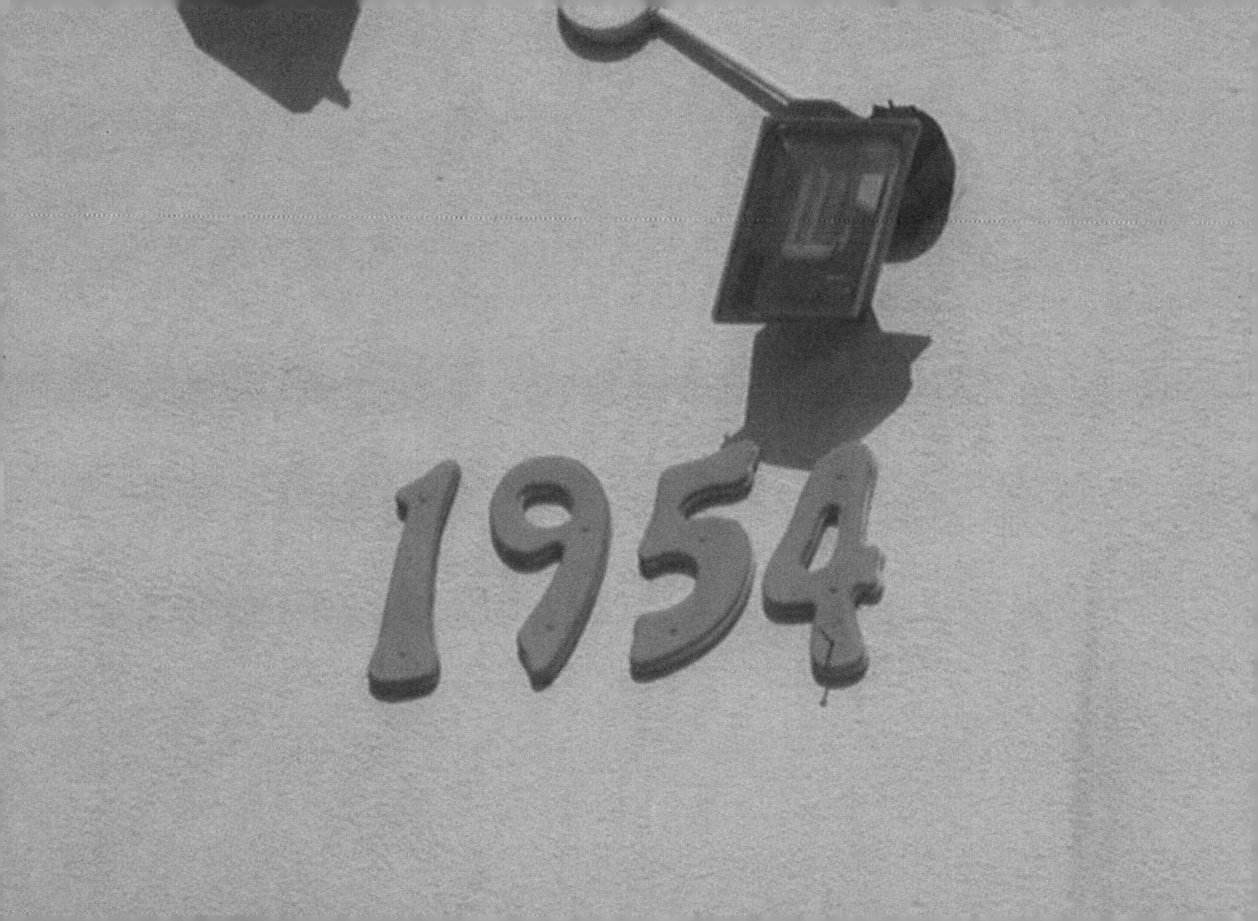
1954

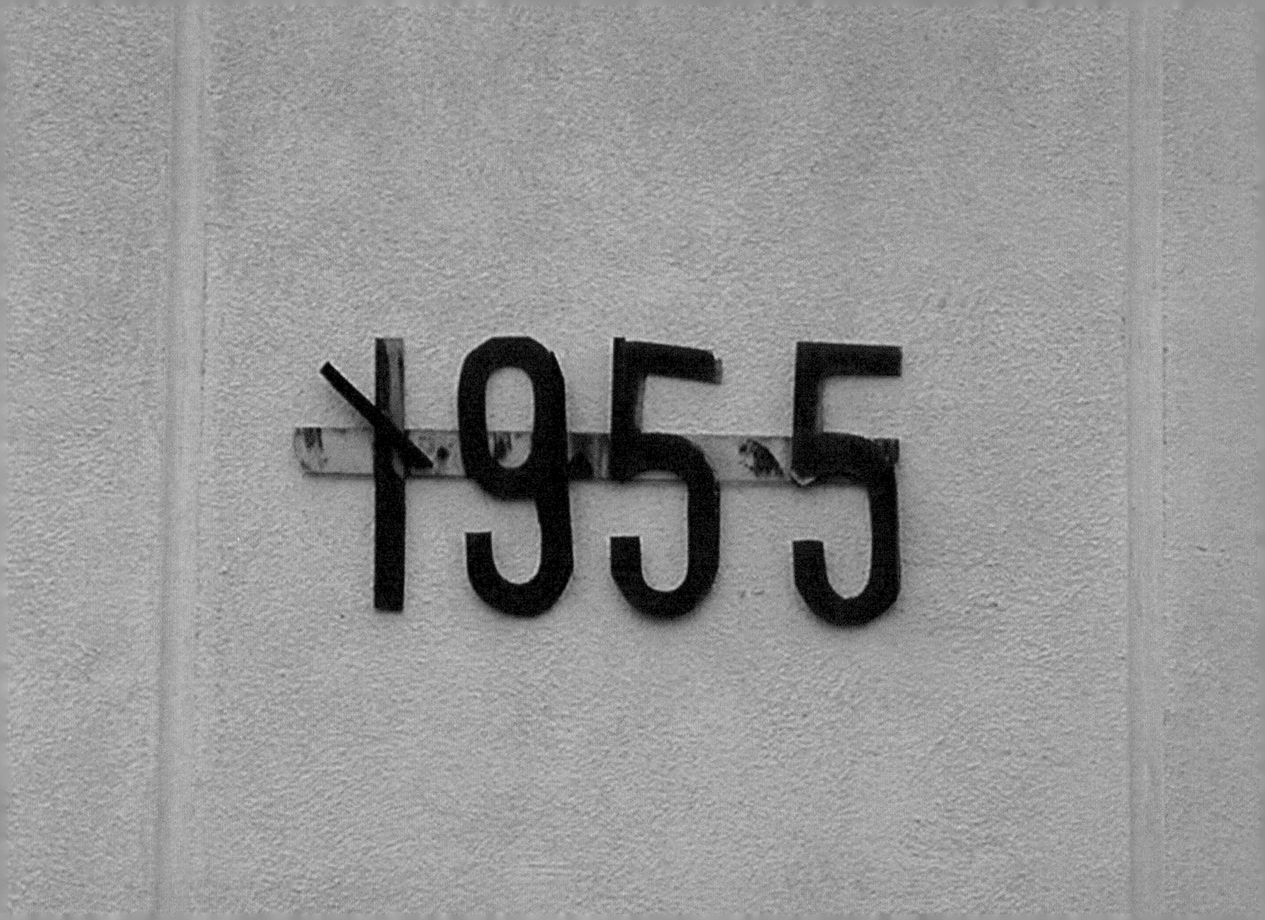
1955

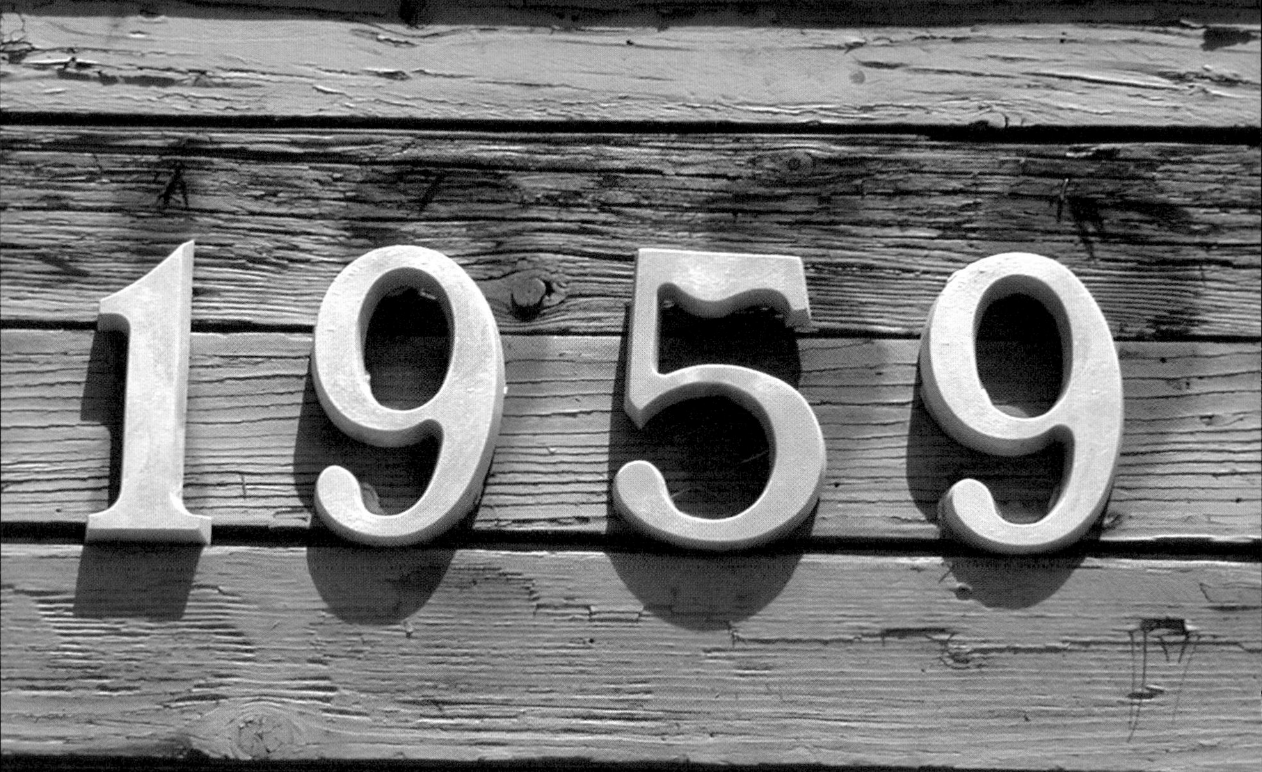
1959

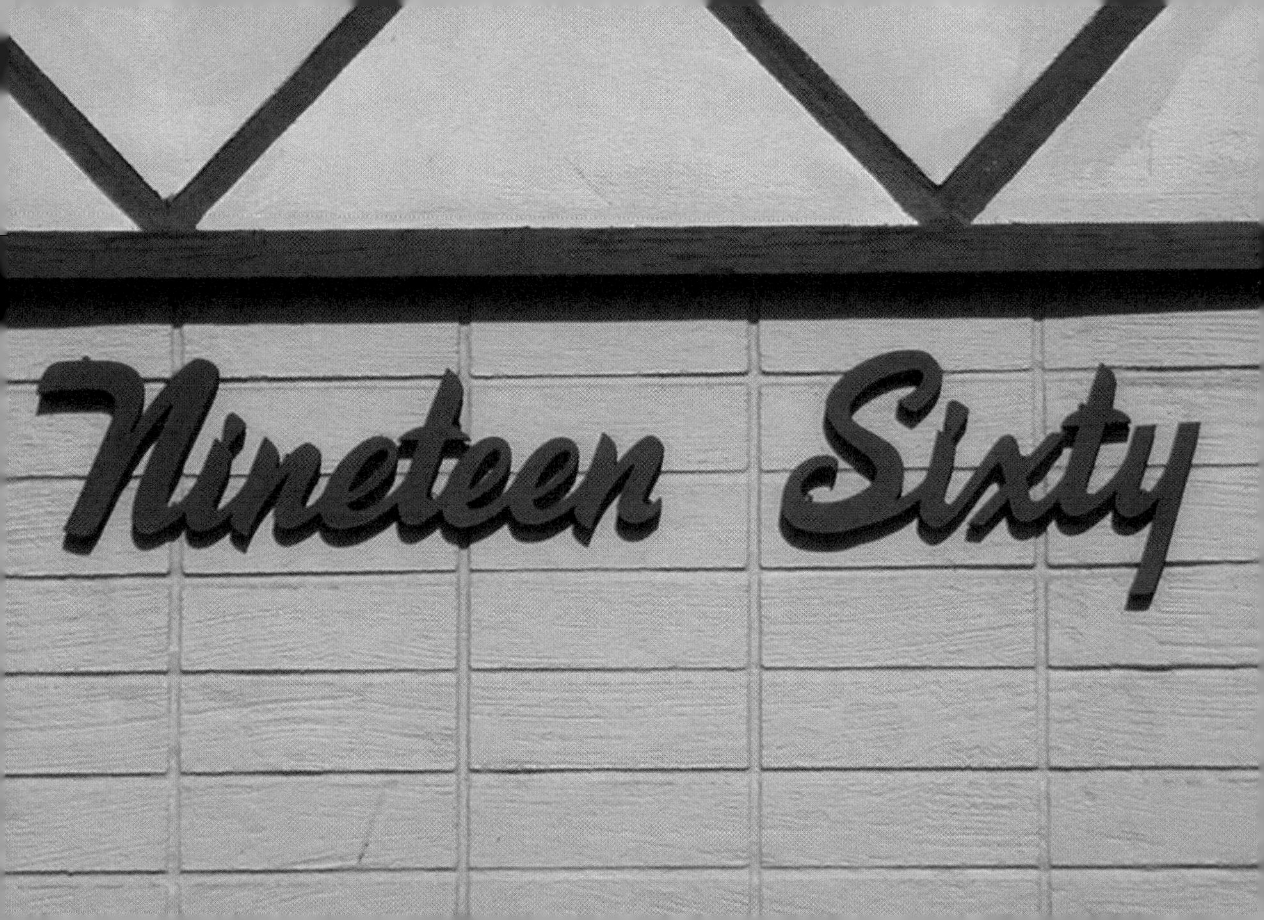
Nineteen Sixty

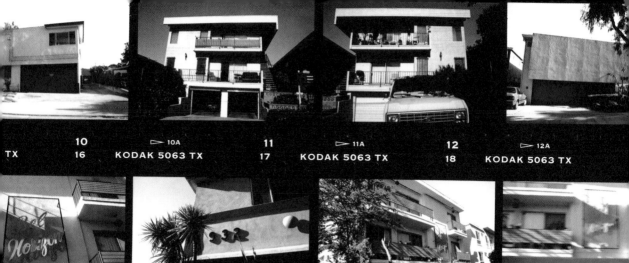

10   10A   11   11A   12   12A
TX   16   KODAK 5063 TX   11   17   KODAK 5063 TX   12   18   KODAK 5063 TX

16   16A   17   17A   18   18A
TX   22   K 5063 TX   17   23   KODAK 5063 TX   18   24   KODAK 5063 TX

32A   33   33A   34   34A   35   35A

5063 TX   21   KODAK 5063 TX   22   KODAK 5063 TX   23   KODAK 5063

20A   21   21A   22   22A   23   23A

5063 TX   9   KODAK 5063 TX   10   KODAK 5063 TX   11   KODAK 5063

2467   2467   BEVERLYWOOD

9   ▷ 9A   10   ▷ 10A   11   ▷ 11A   12

15   KODAK 5053 TMY   16   KODAK 5053 TMY   17   KODAK 5053 TMY   18

15   ▷ 15A   16   ▷ 16A   17   ▷ 17A   18

21   KODAK 5053 TMY   22   KODAK 5053 TMY   23   KODAK 5053 TMY   24

2   ▷ 2A   3   ▷ 3A   4   ▷ 4A

3 TX   8   KODAK 5063 TX   9   KODAK 5063 TX   10   KODAK 5063 TX

8   ▷ 8A   9   ▷ 9A   10   ▷ 10A

TX   14   KODAK 5063 TX   15   KODAK 5063 TX   16   KODAK 5063 TX

9   ▷ 9A   10   ▷ 10A   11   ▷ 11A

53 TMY   15   KODAK 5053 TMY   16   KODAK 5053 TMY   17   KODAK 5053 TMY

A   15   ▷ 15A   16   ▷ 16A   17   ▷ 17A

53 TMY   21   KODAK 5053 TMY   22   KODAK 5053 TMY   23   KODAK 5053 TMY

One One Two Nine Six Brookhaven

Seafoam Apartments

1234

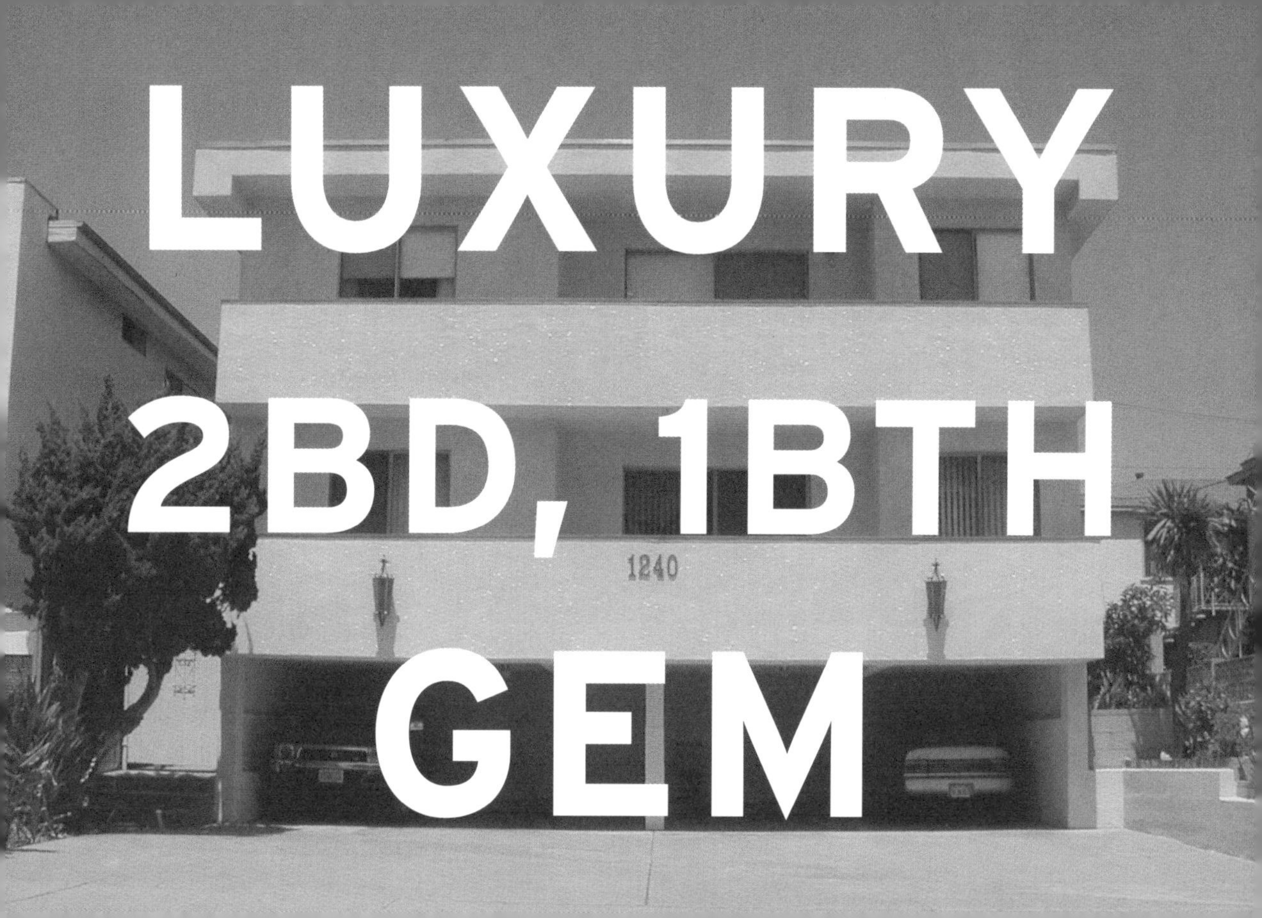

LUXURY
2BD, 1BTH
GEM
1240

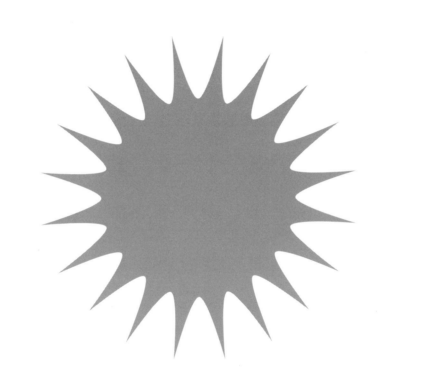

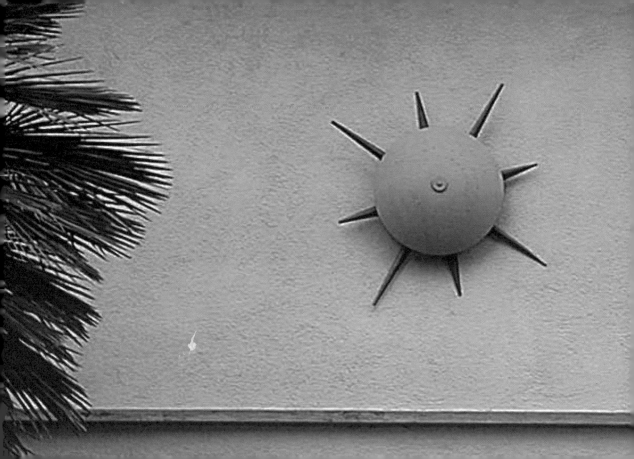

ONE
BEDROOM
★ POOL ★

One Two Three
CALIFORNIA

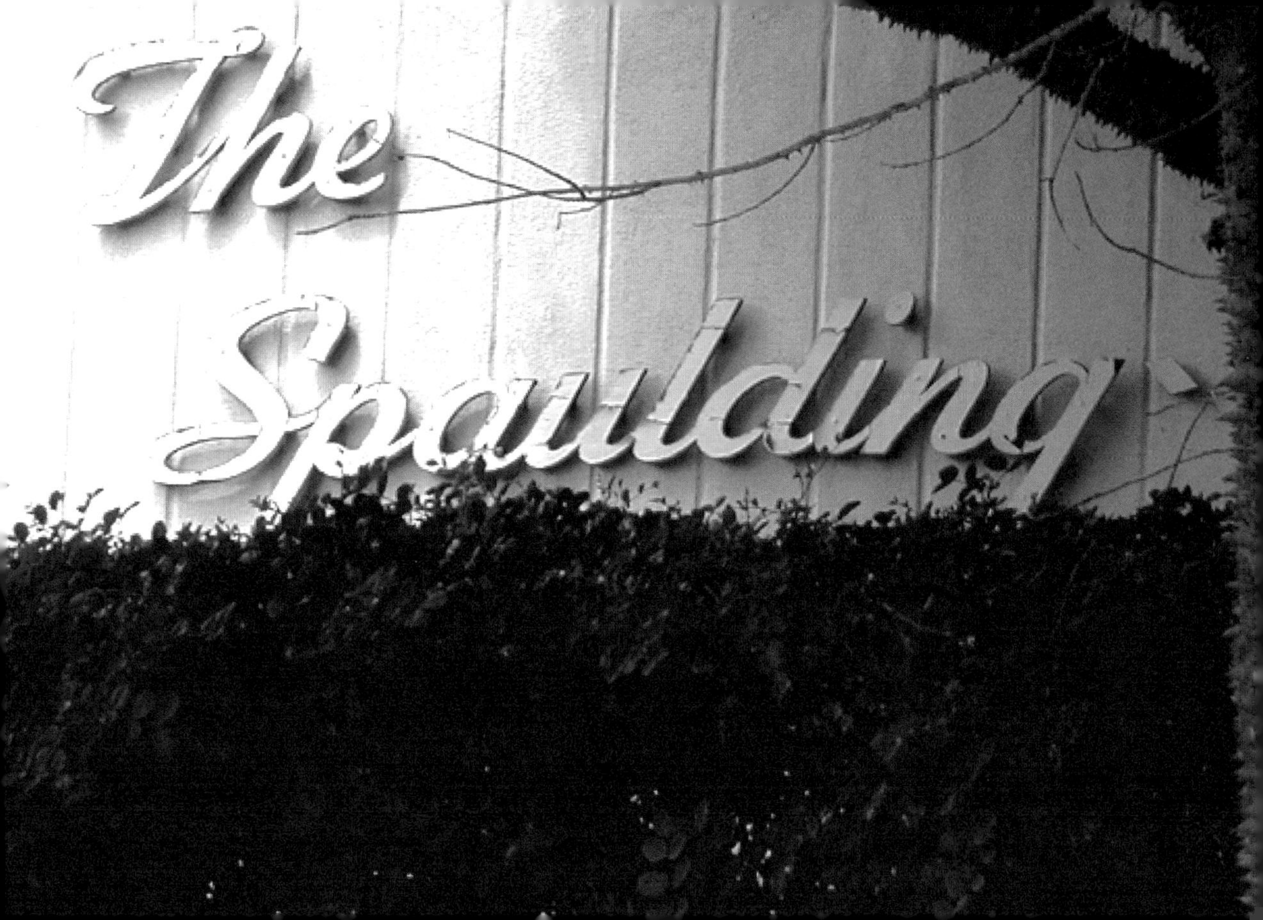
The Spaulding

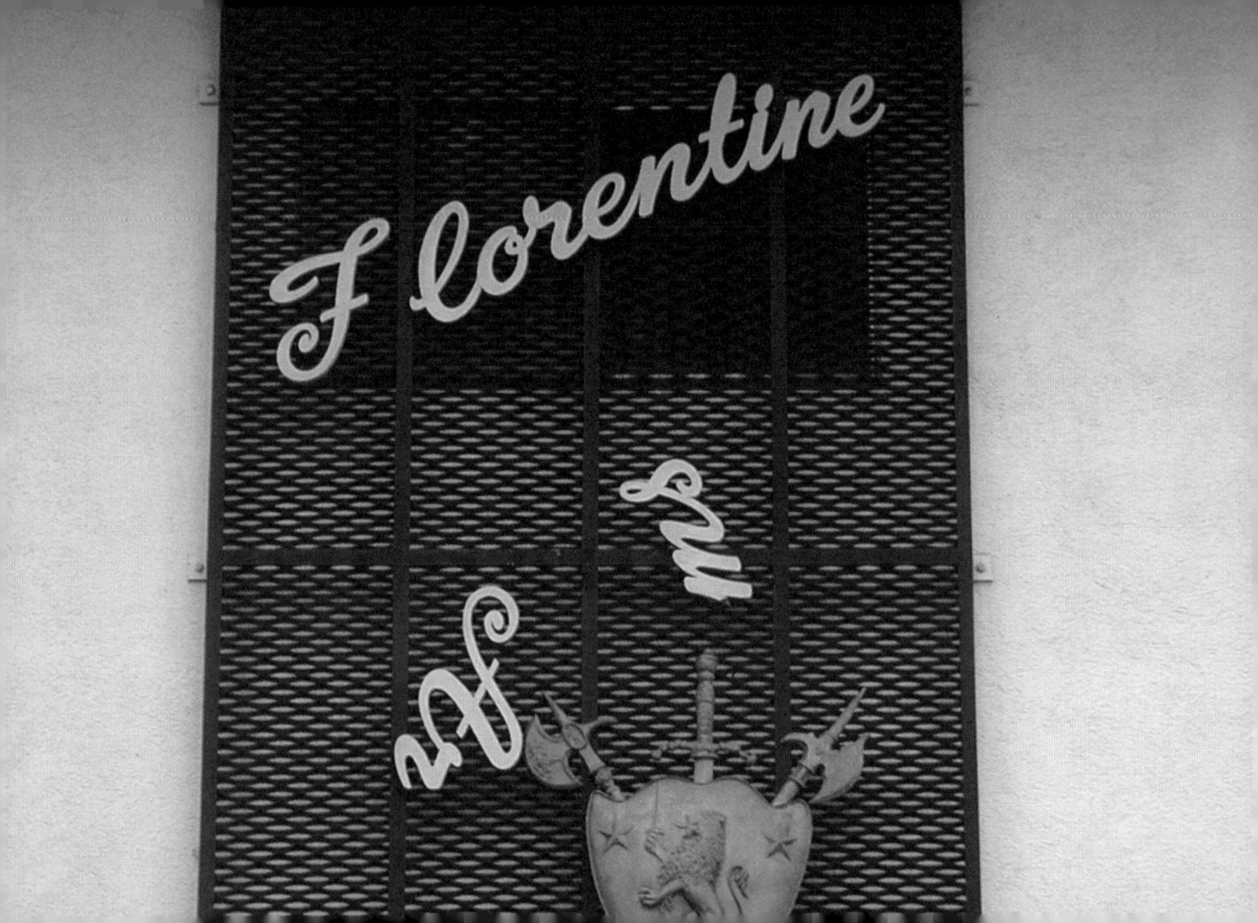
Florentine

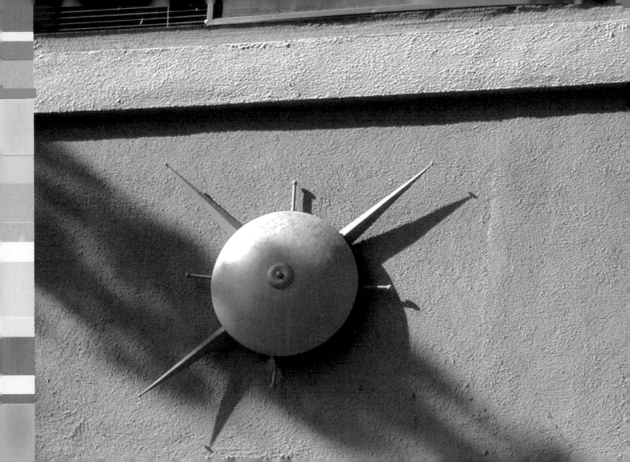

THE *Bahamas* APTS.

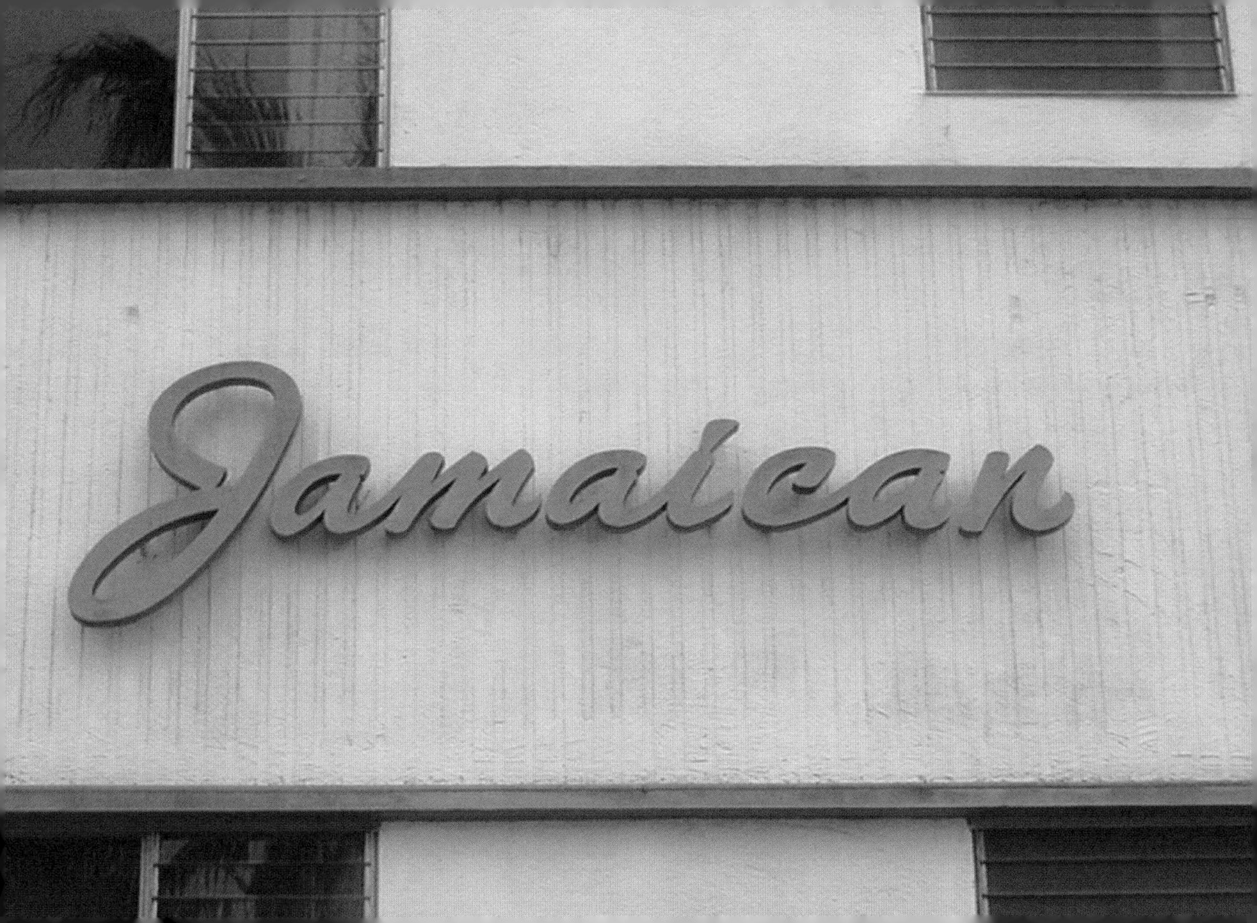
Jamaican

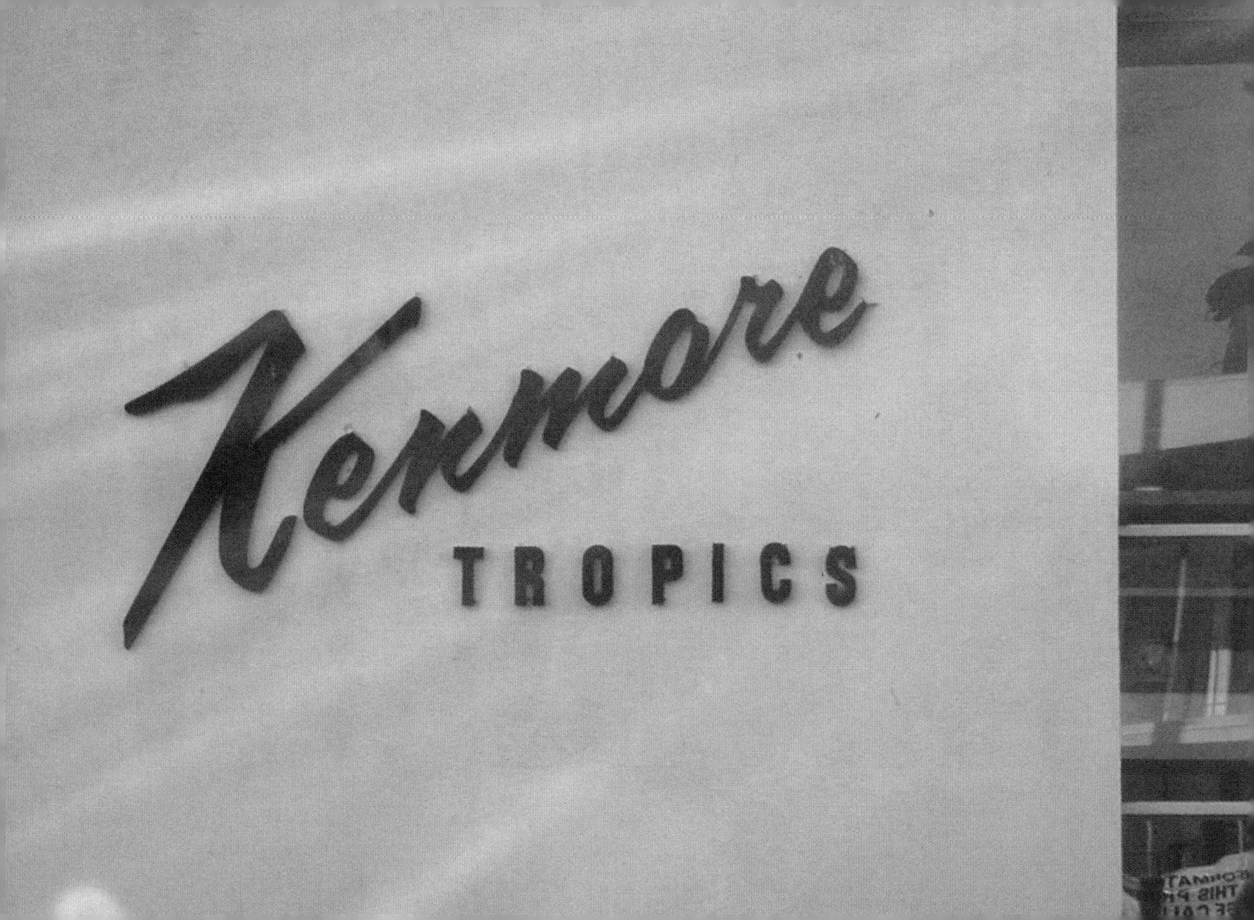
Kenmore
TROPICS

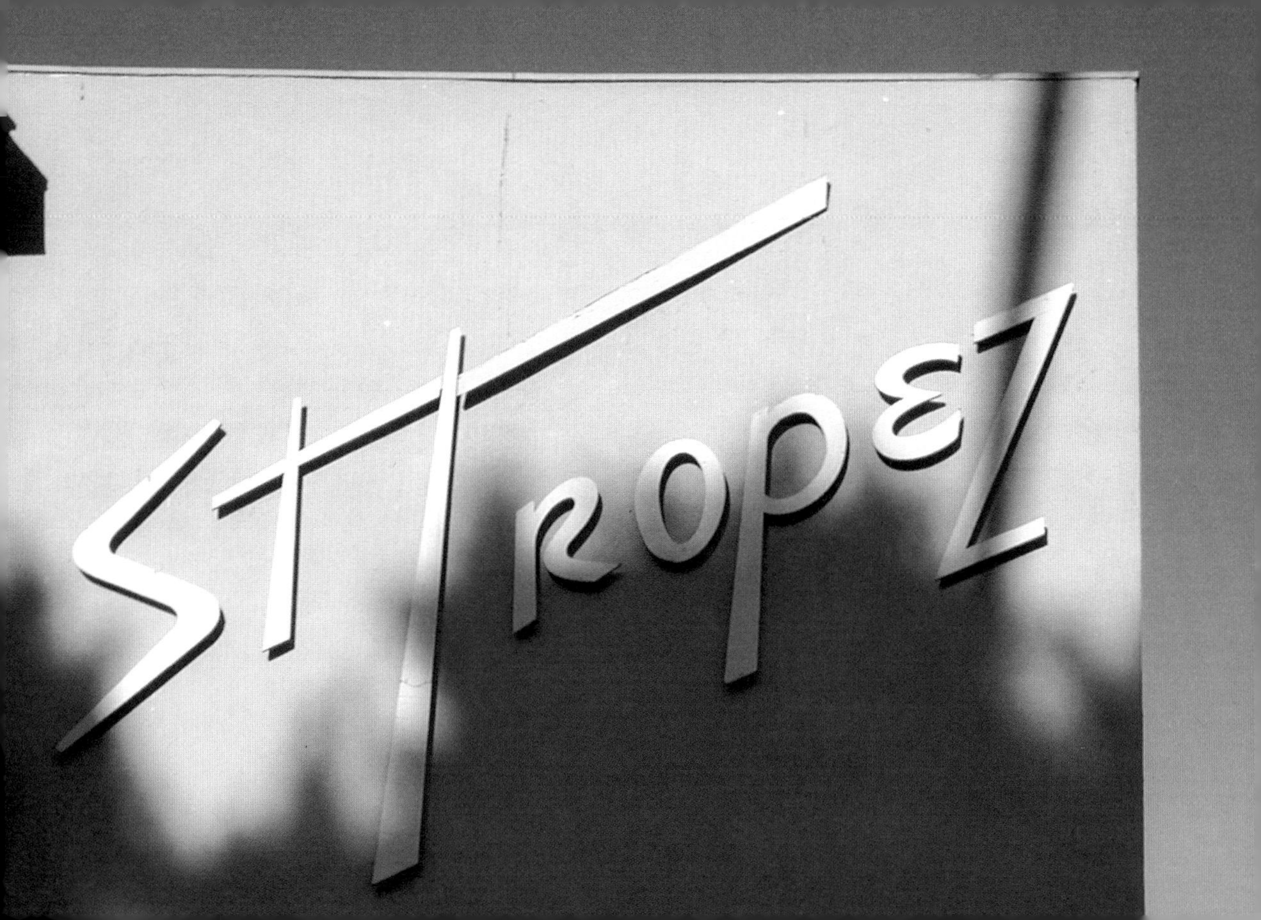
St Tropez

Five O

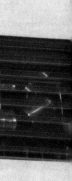

Ten
Twenty

Ten Forty S

Eighteen Twenty Eight

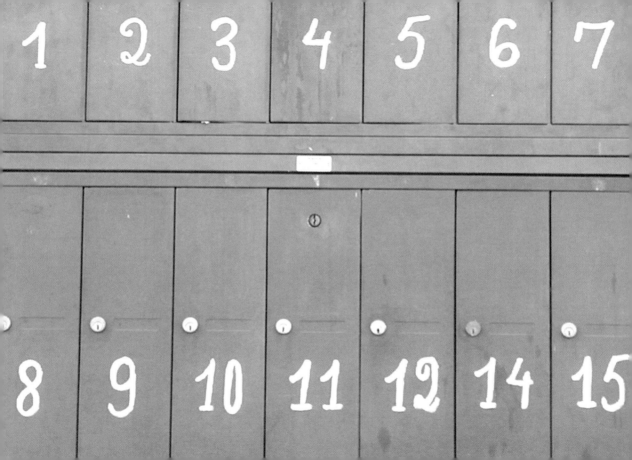

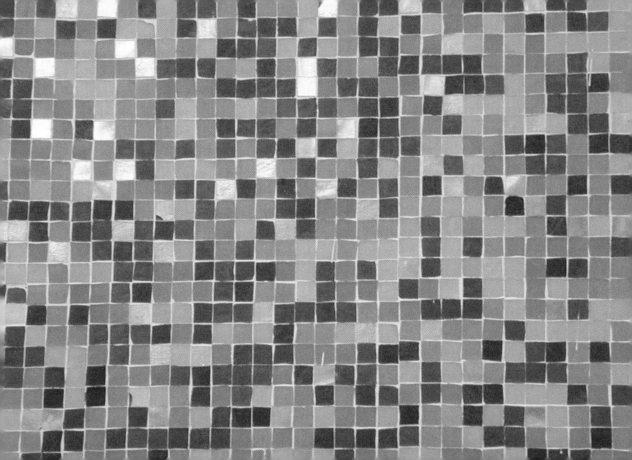

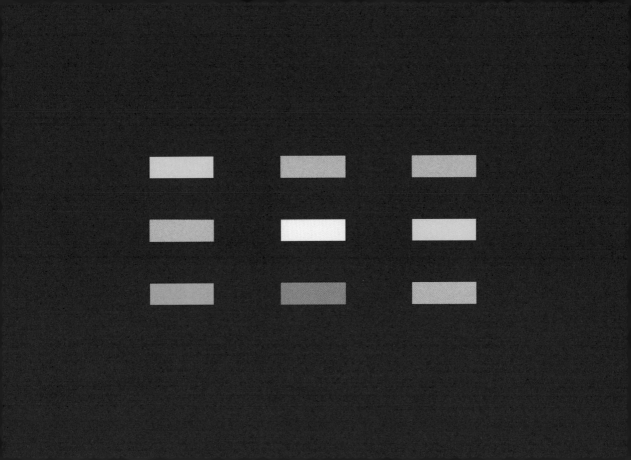

DELUXE,
2BD, 1.75 BTH
FURNISHED

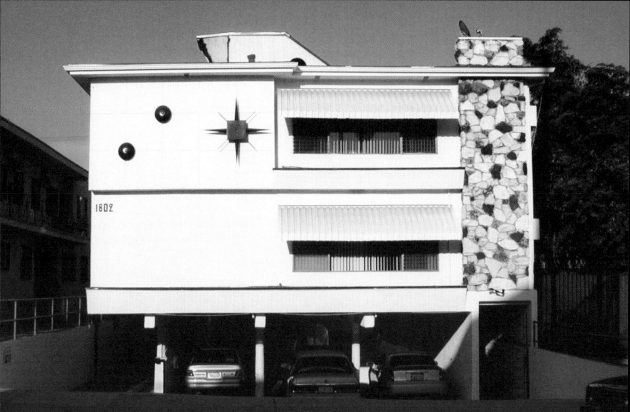

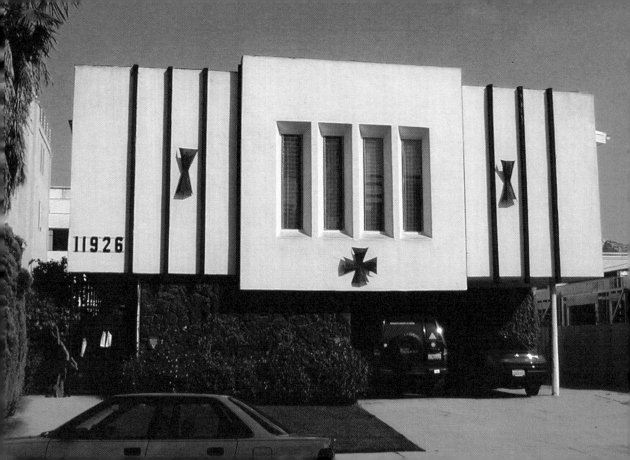

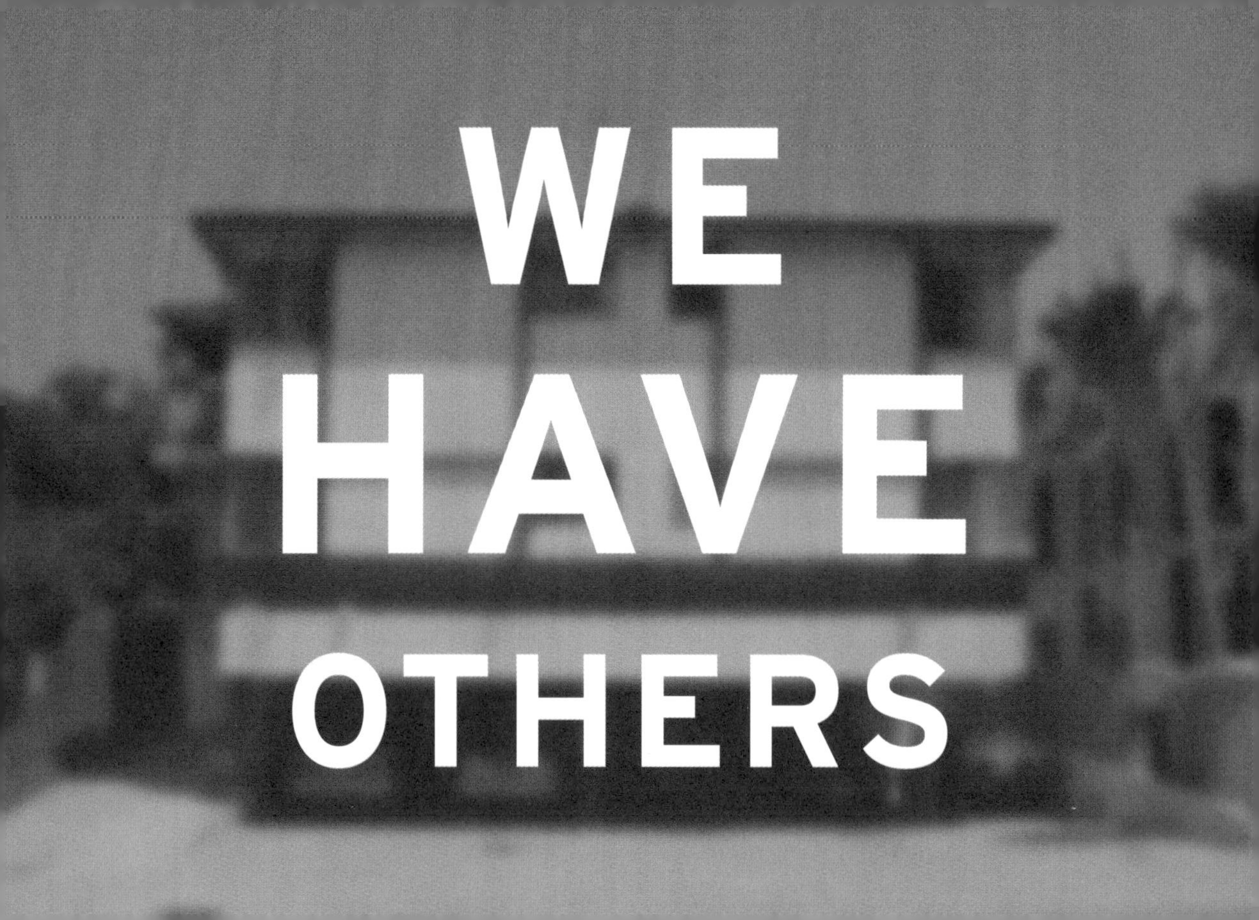
WE
HAVE
OTHERS

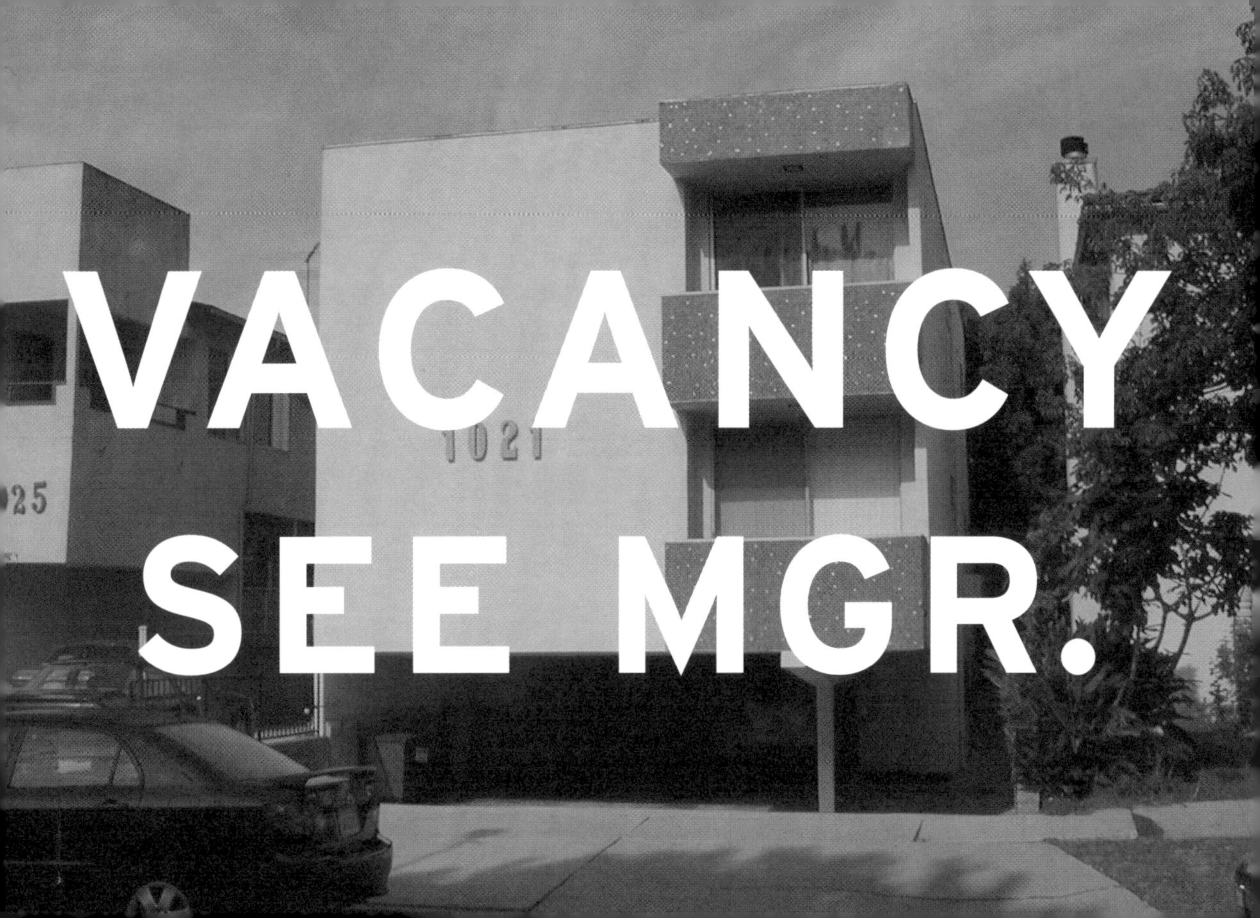
VACANCY
SEE MGR.
1021

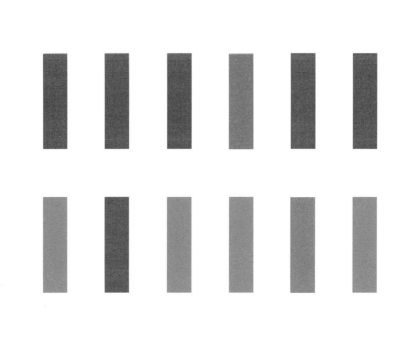

TENANT PARKING ONLY

VIOLATORS WILL BE CITED AND

TOWED AWAY

AT VEHICLE OWNERS EXPENSE

C.V.C. 22658A POLICE

Teri·Lyn

252

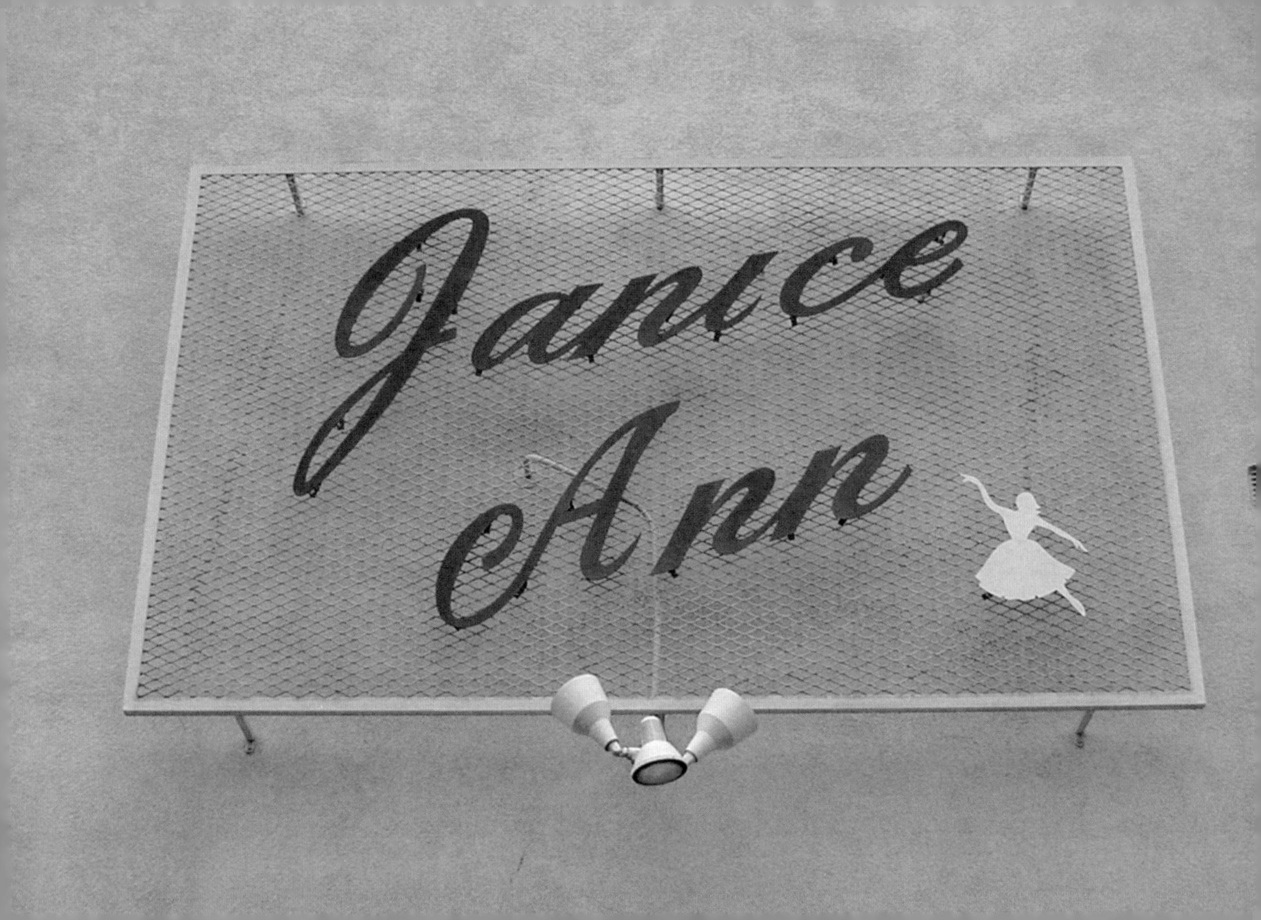
Janice
Ann

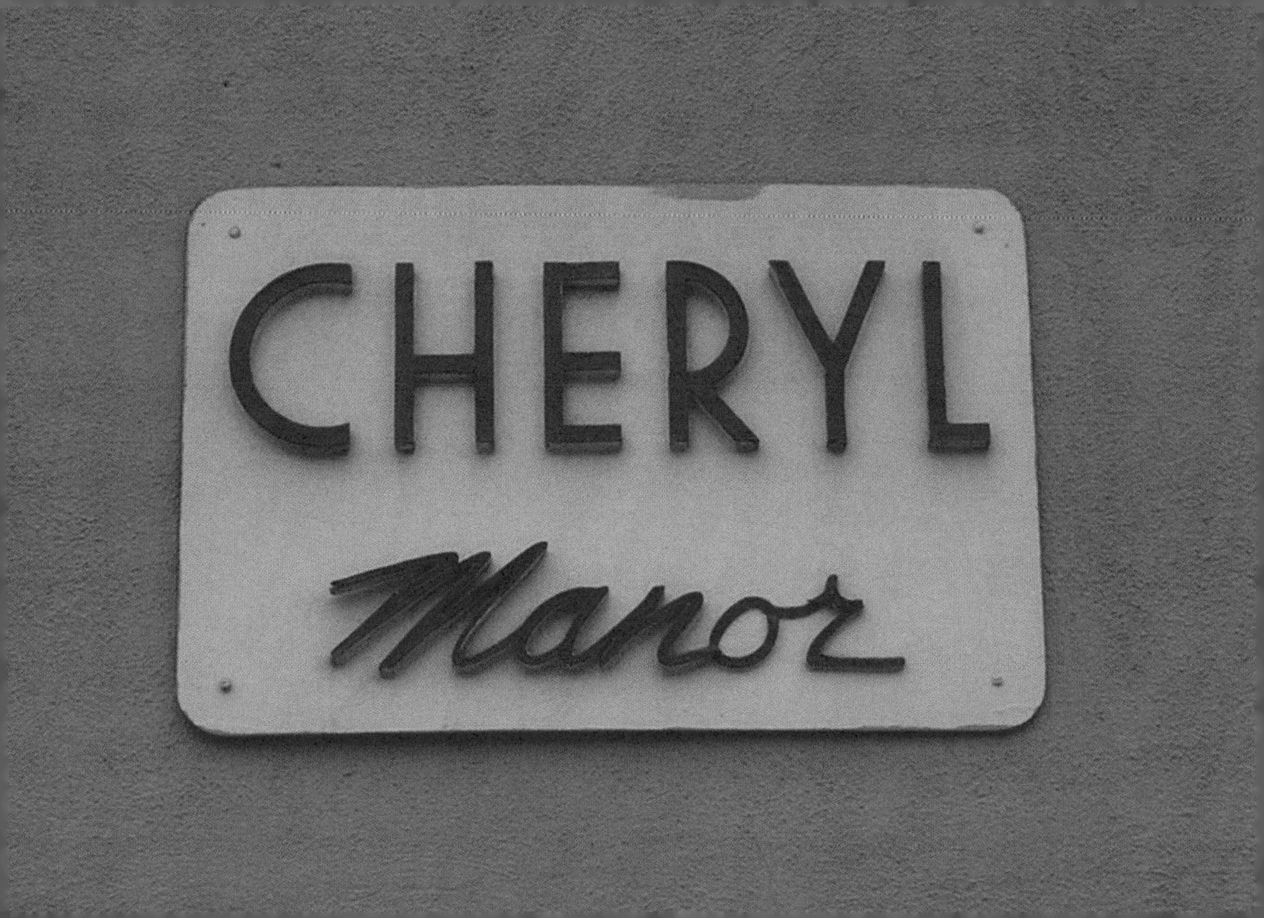
CHERYL
Manor

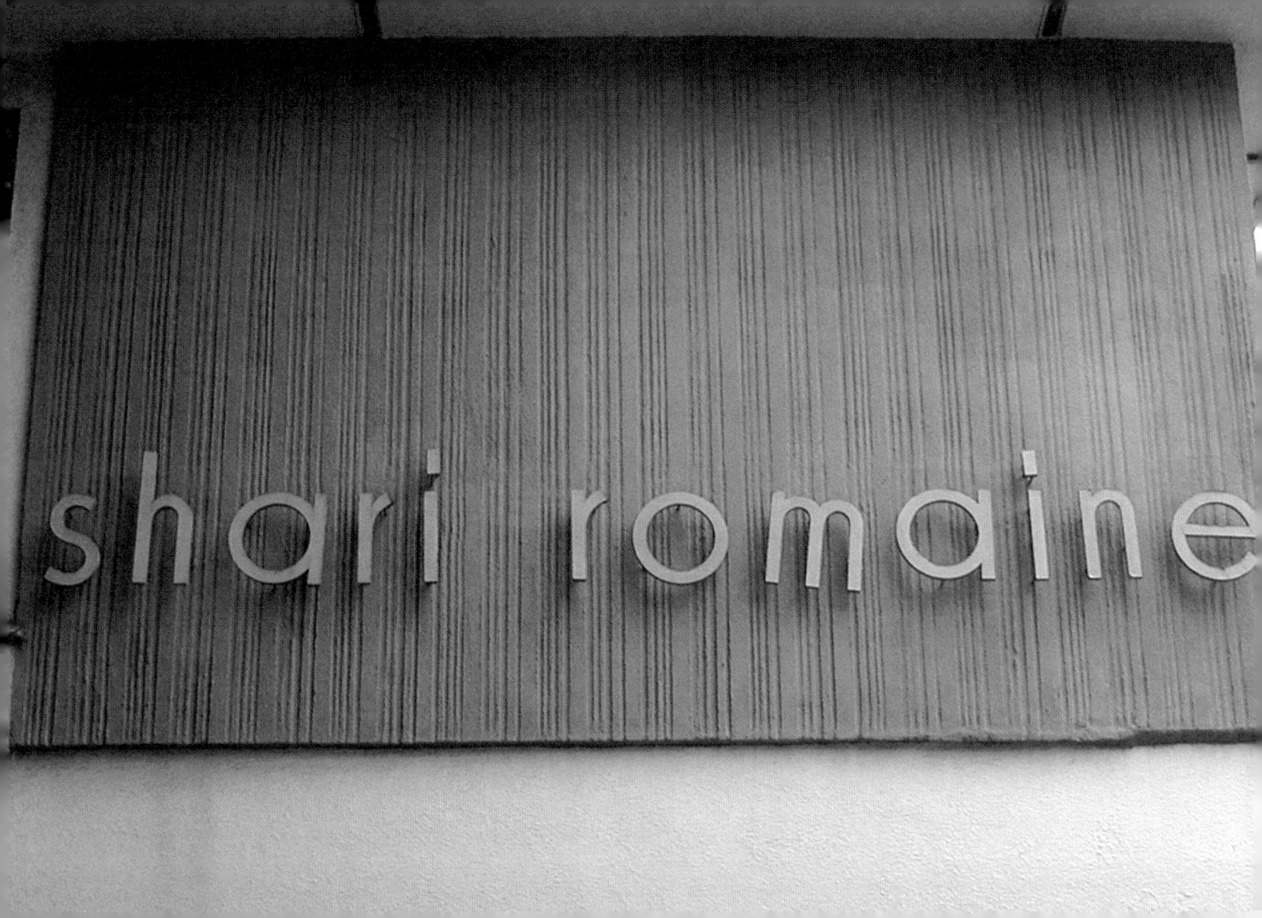
shari romaine

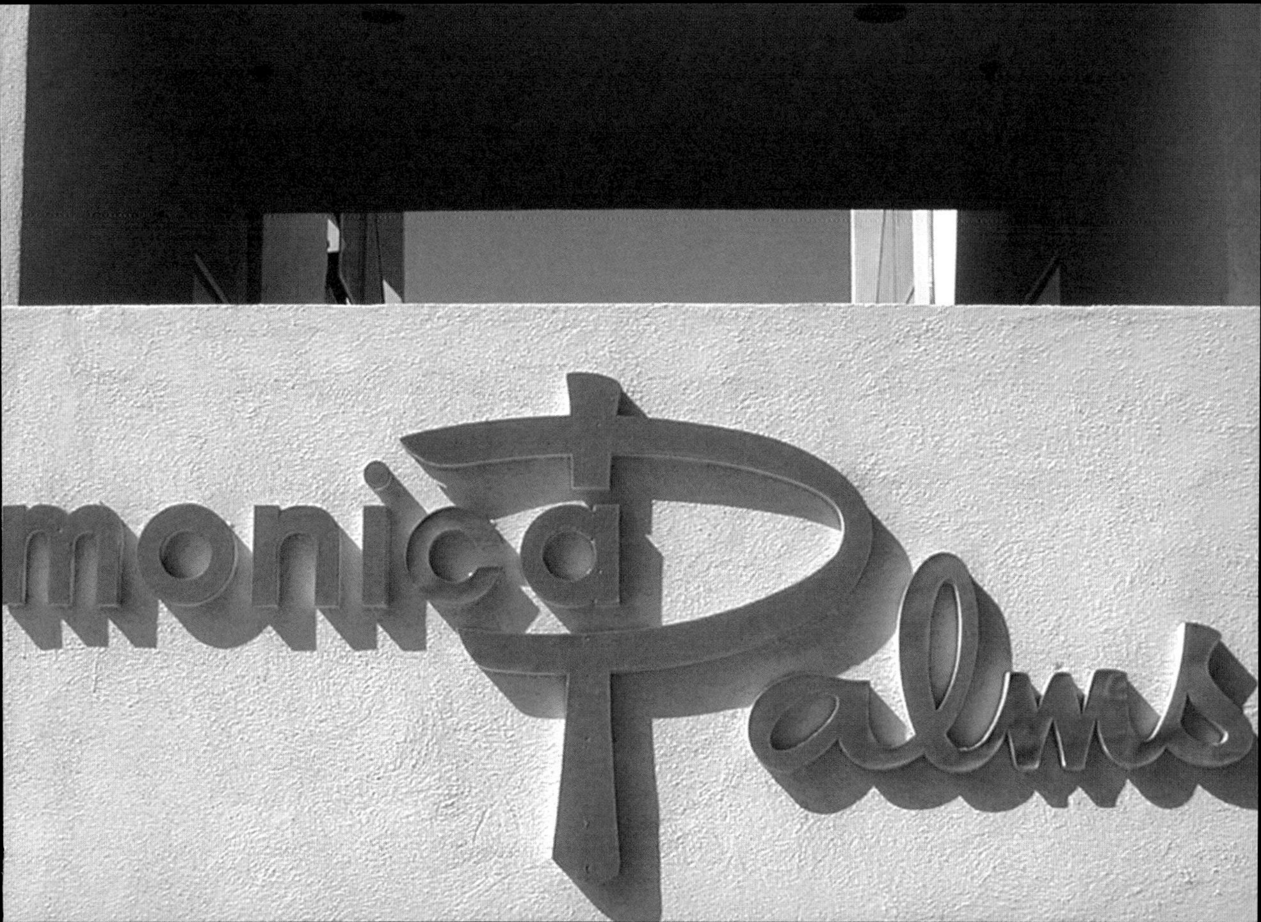
monica Palms

Den

THE
Ocean View
202

South

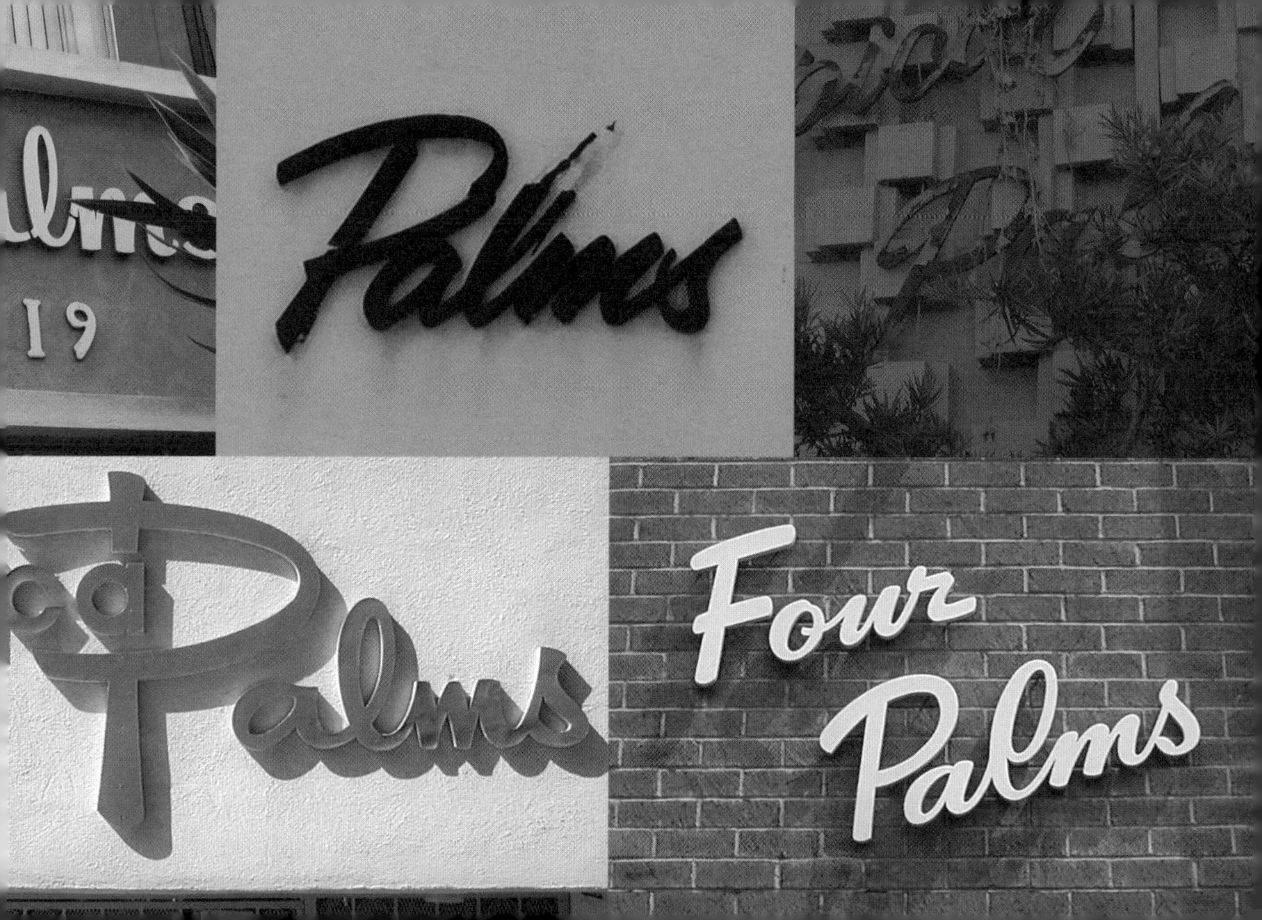

Sherbourne West

SHERBOURNE
Cadillac

Sherbourne
TERRACE

Sherbourne
de Ville

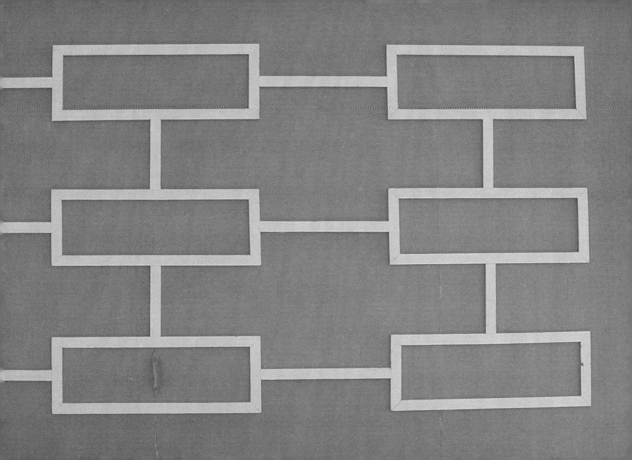

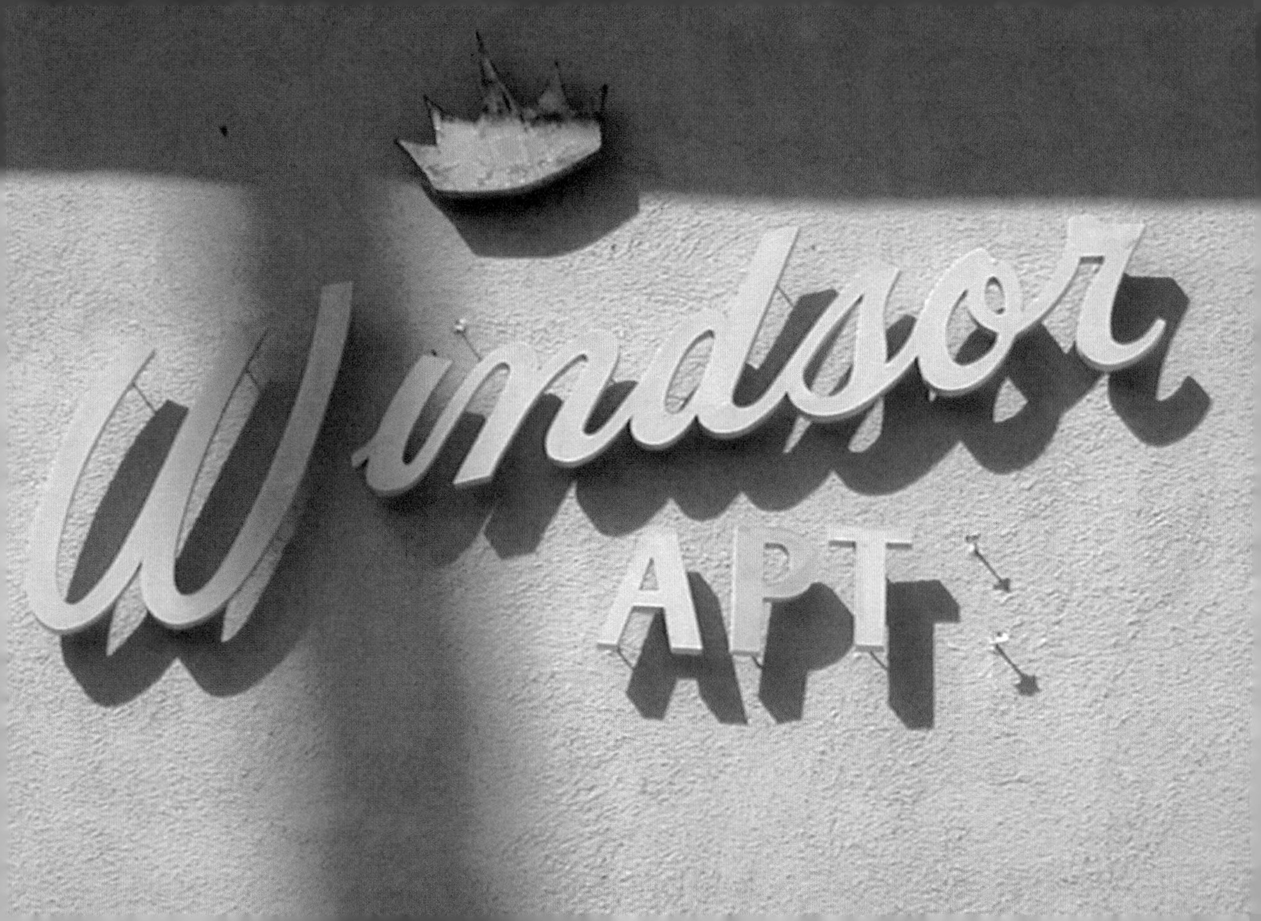
Windsor
APT

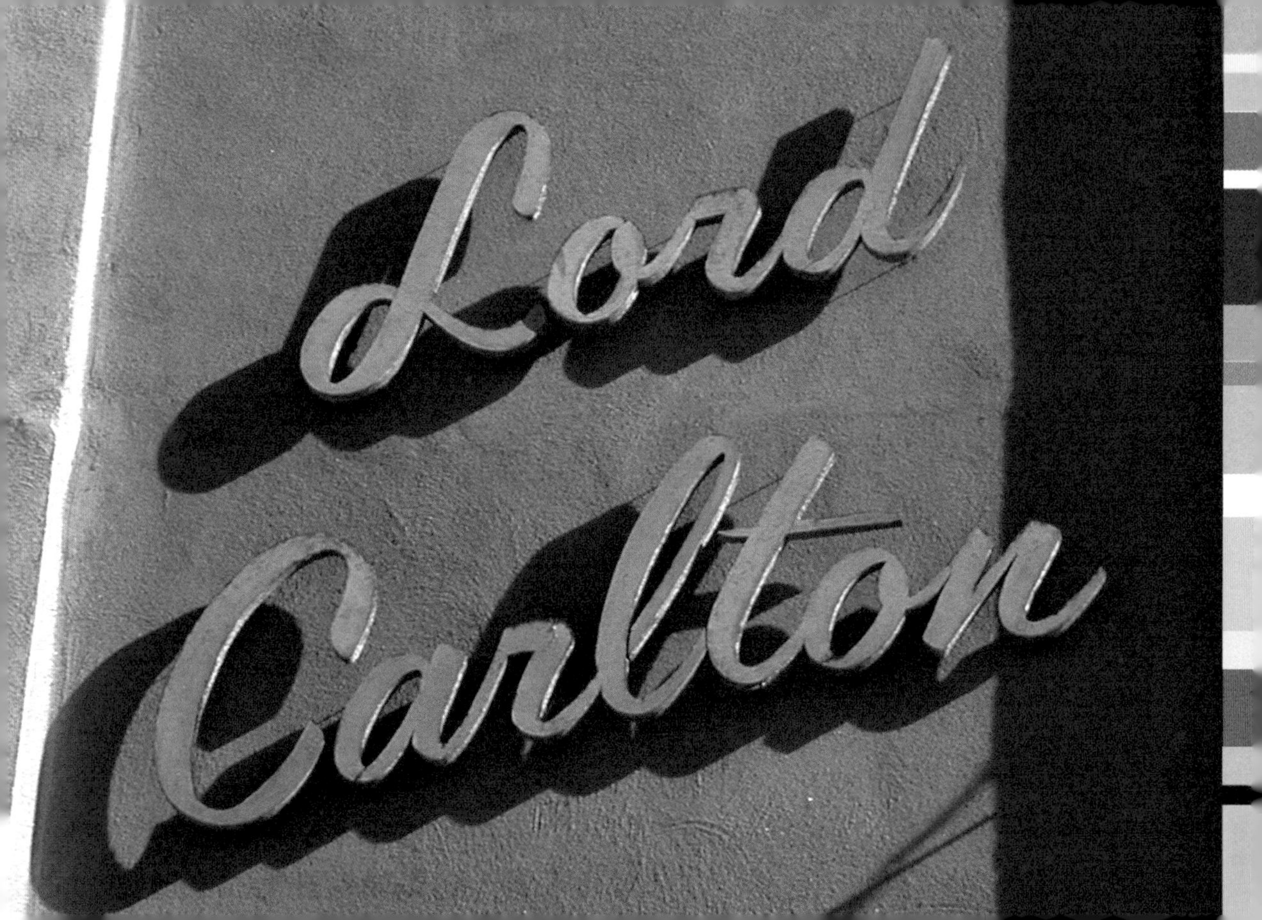
Lord
Carlton

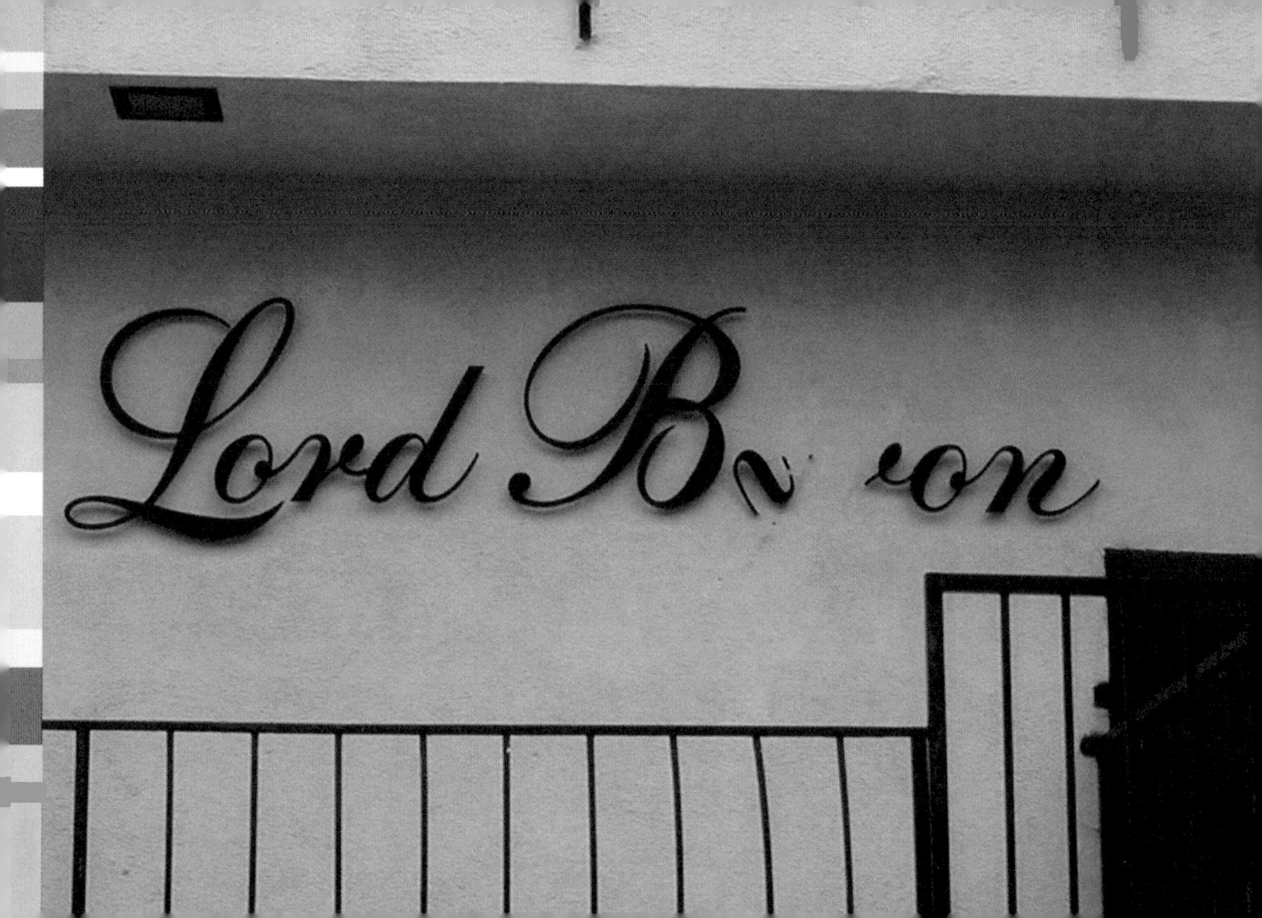
Lord B ron

Wilton
MANOR

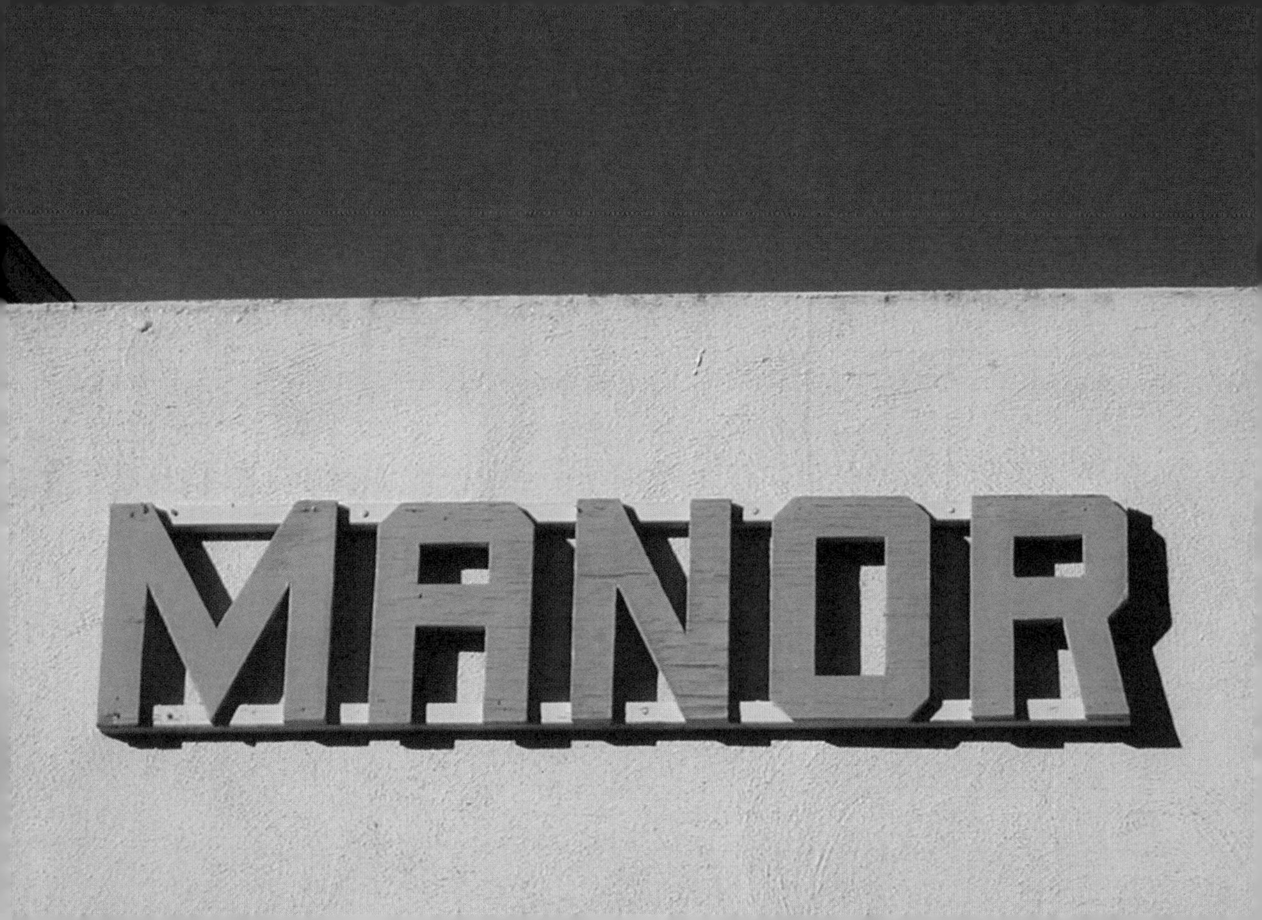
MANOR

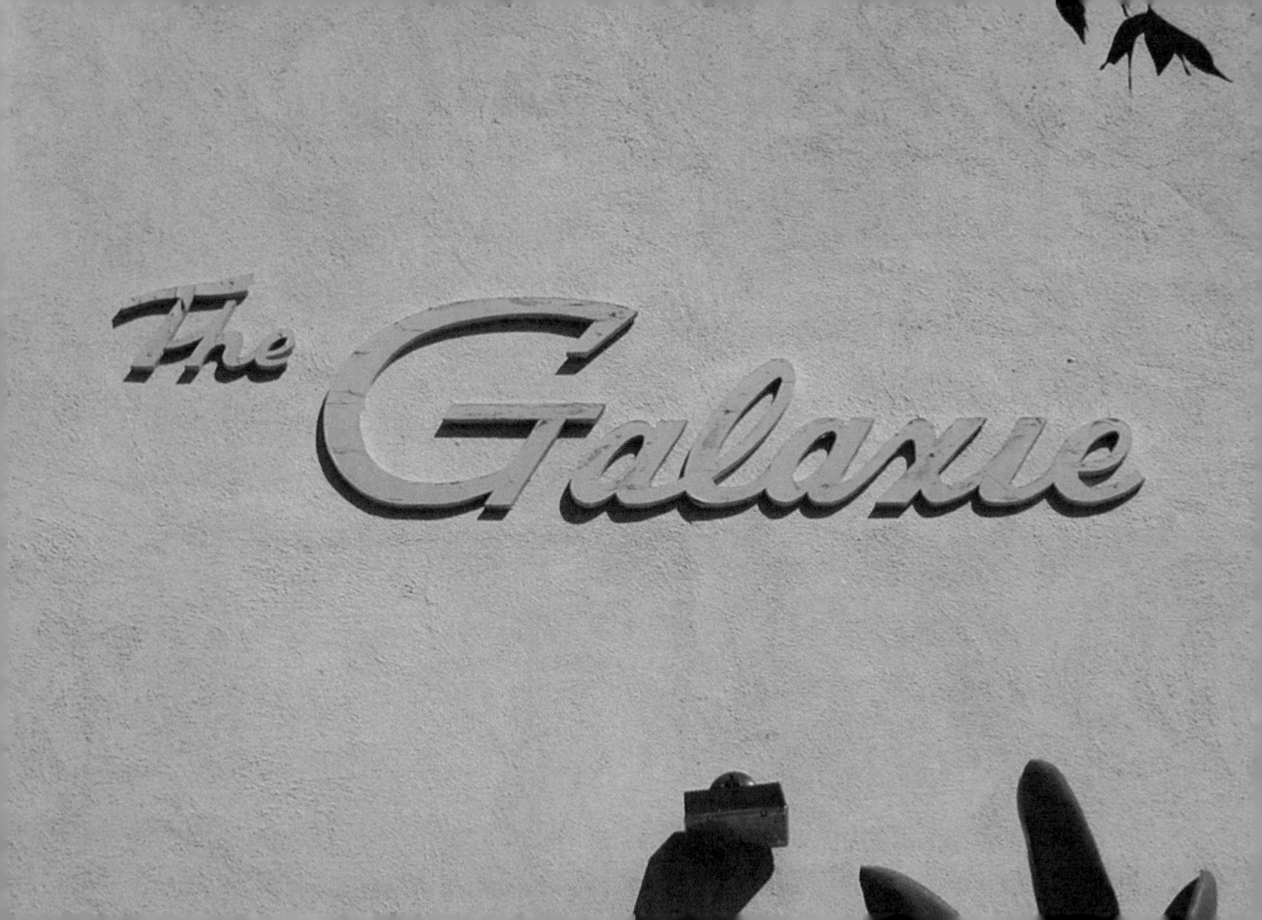
The Galaxie

BOURNE

Cadillac

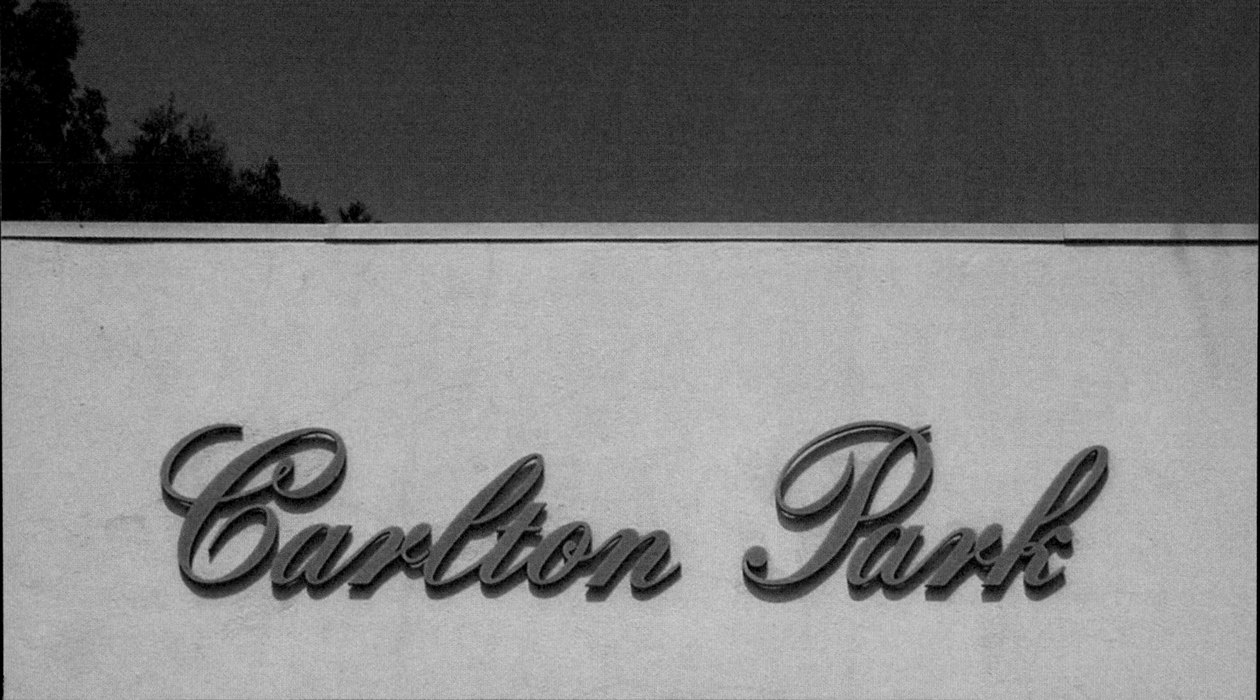
Carlton Park

one o one

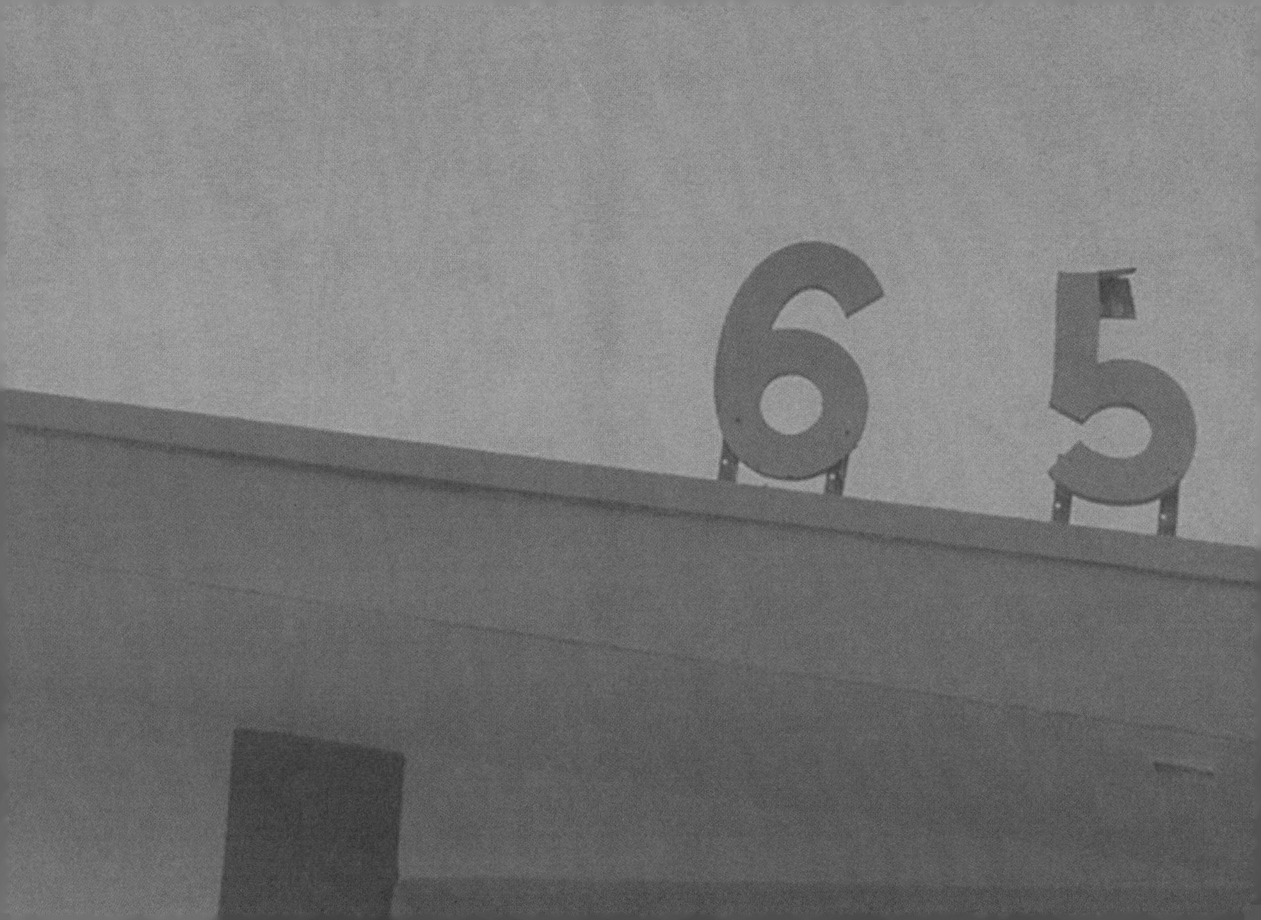
6 5

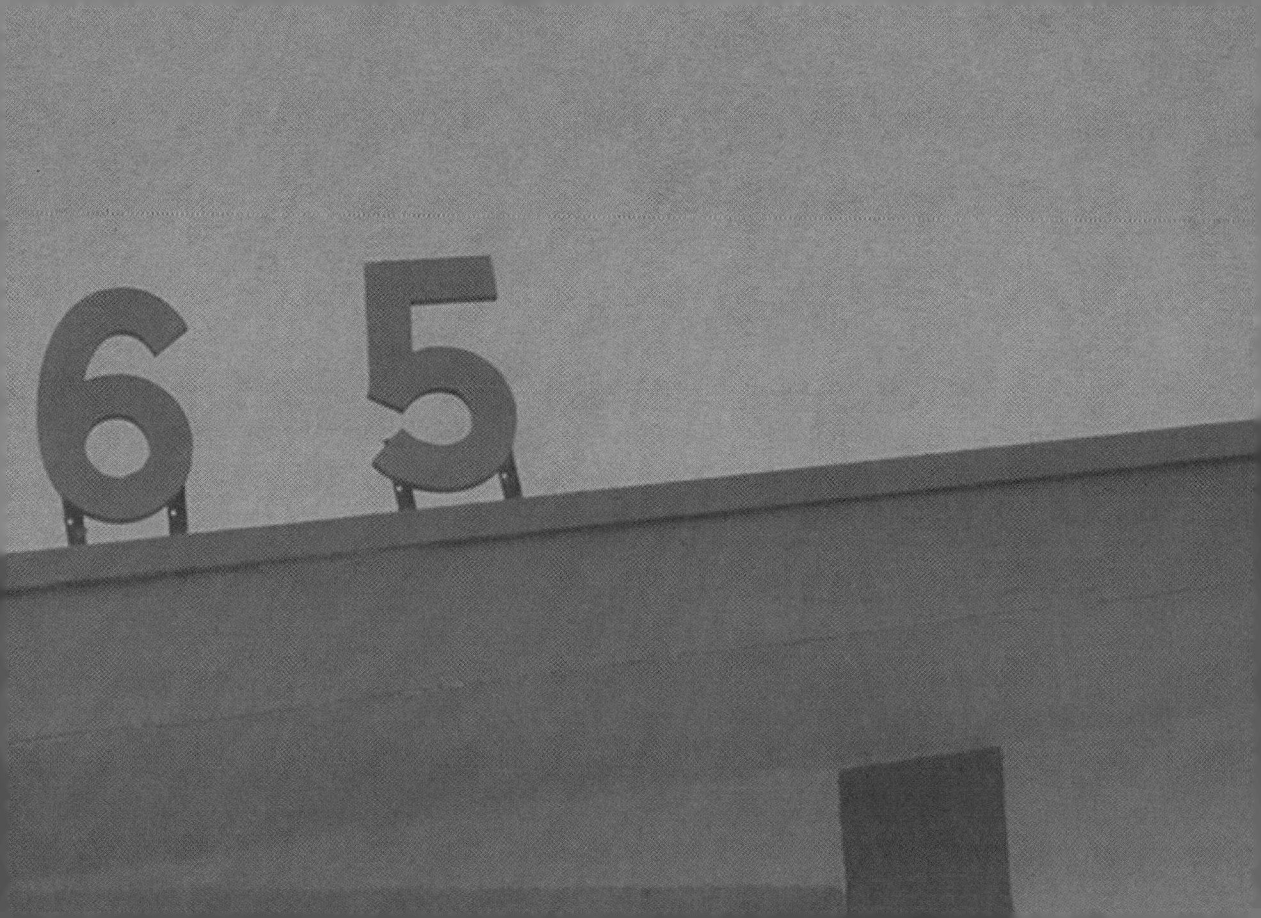
6 5

NO
PARKING

UNAUTHORIZED VEHICLES
WILL BE TOWED AWAY AT
VEHICLE OWNERS EXPENSE
POLICE PH. 855-8850   C.V.C. 22658A

3 BEDROOMS

APARTMENT
FOR RENT

310 836-5006

SHOWN BY
APPOINTMENT Only

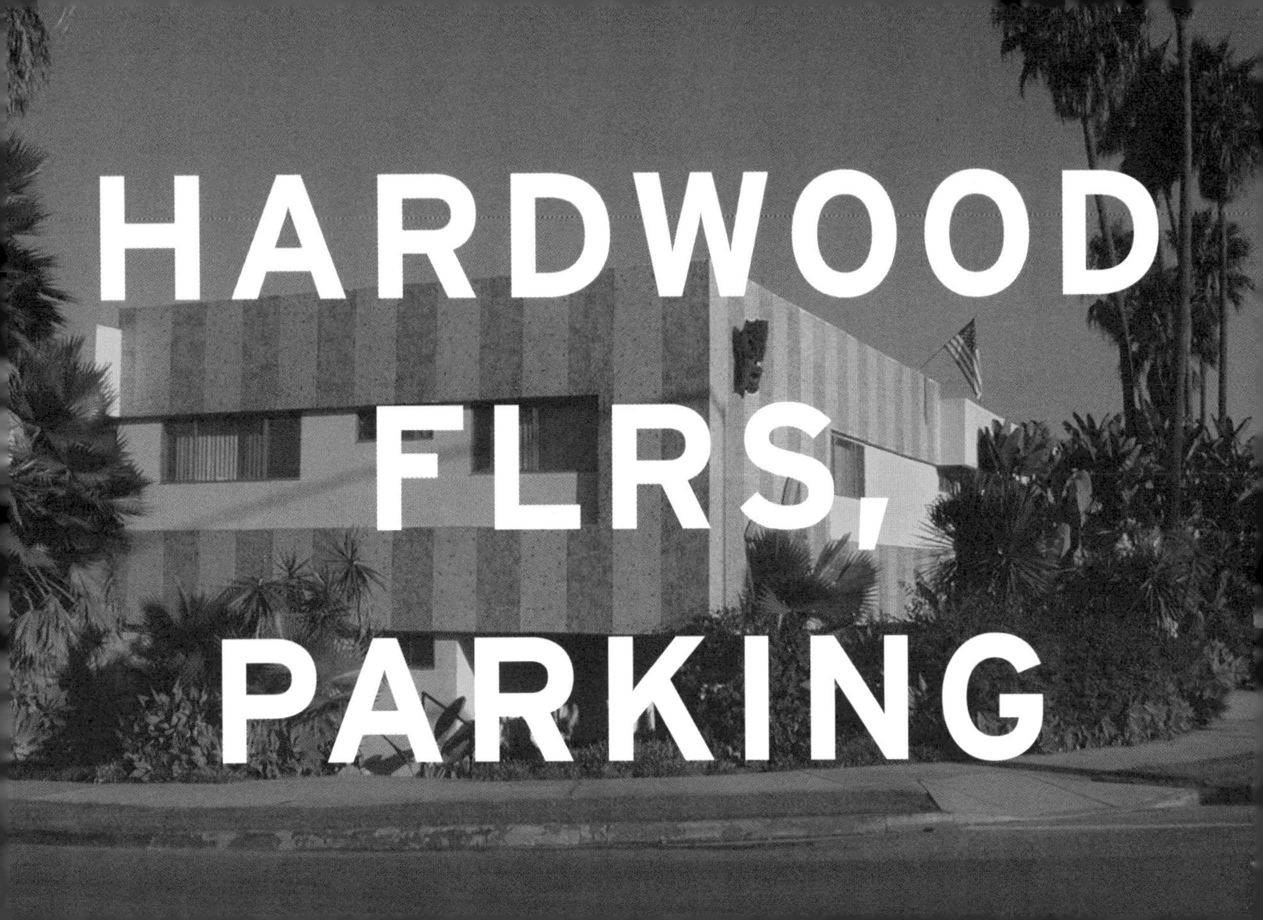
HARDWOOD
FLRS,
PARKING

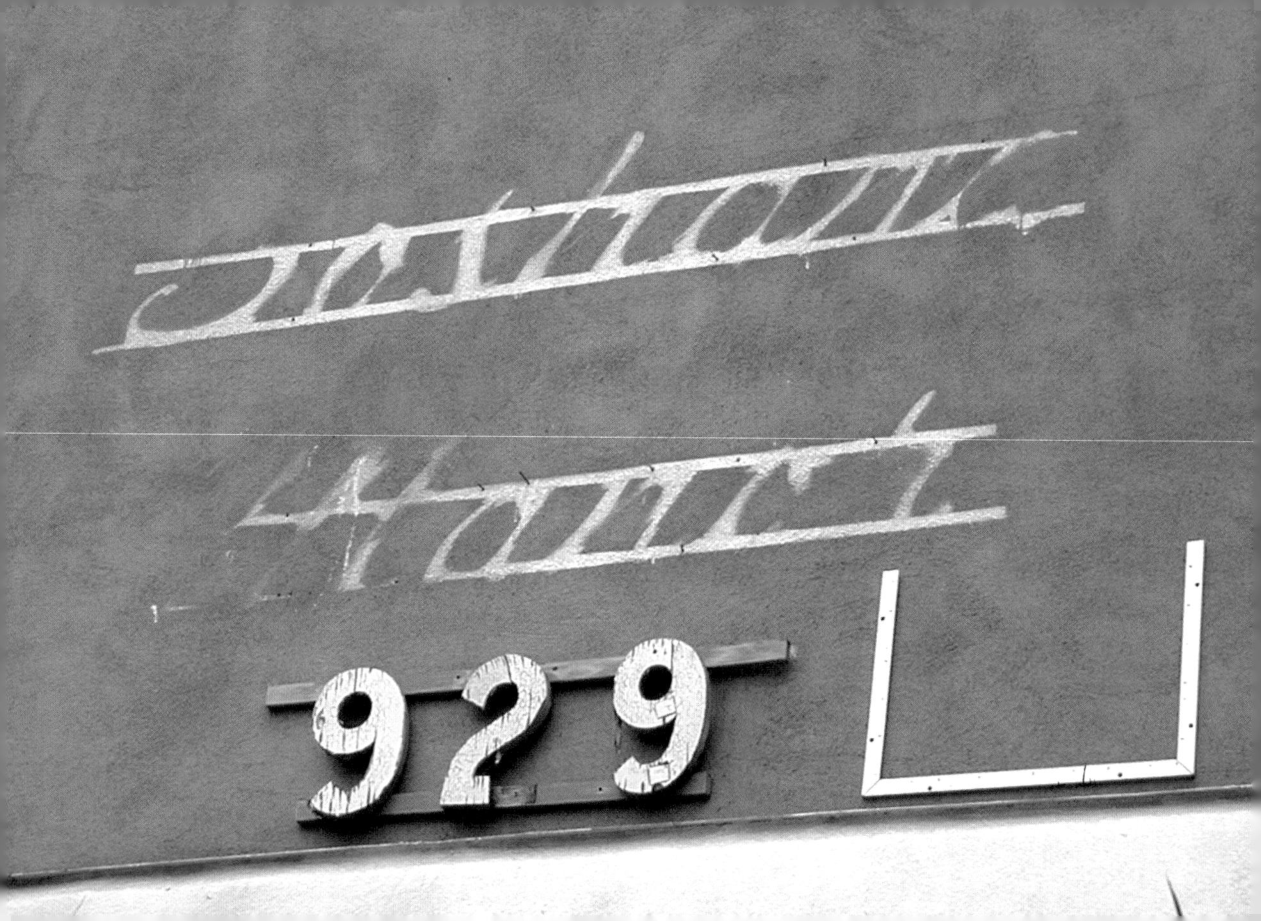
929

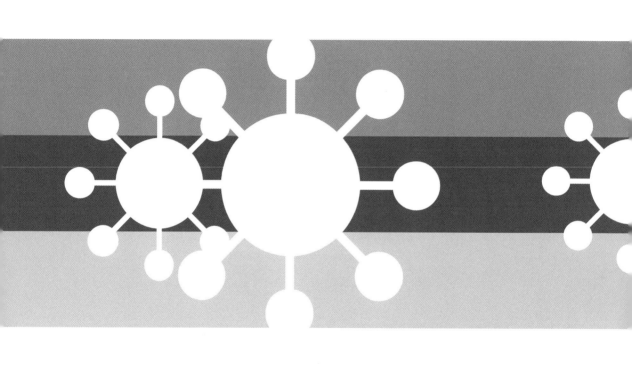

The text for this book (what little there is) is set in News Gothic, designed by Morris Benton in 1908 and **INTERSTATE**, designed by Tobias Frere-Jones in 1994.

My thanks to Alan Rapp at Chronicle for all of his gentle, good guidance. Everyone at Ph.D, especially my partner Michael. To Mick Brownfield, Rod Dyer, Jim Heimann and Ed Ruscha. And to three designers whose profound greatness continues to inspire: Rudy Vanderlans, Mick Haggarty, and "The Shortstop" Mike Fink. And, of course, Annie.

Clive Piercy is a partner and creative director of Ph.D, an award-winning graphic design studio in Santa Monica, California. He's married to the illustrator Ann Field, and is a lifelong supporter of Tottenham Hotspur FC.

I RETURN AGAIN AND AGAIN TO THE SAM
SENSE OF EXPECTATION WHEN I TURN OI
DINGBAT IN THE DISTANCE. THIS IS NOT
PHOTOGRAPHY. IT IS A VISUAL POEM, A
TO HELP PRESERVE THESE FANTASTIC, C